THE SAN FRANCISCO 49ERS

AN ILLUSTRATED TIMELINE

The San Francisco 49ers face the Cincinnati Bengals in Super Bowl XVI, January 1982.
COURTESY OF GEORGE GOJKOVICH/GETTY IMAGES

THE SAN FRANCISCO 49ERS

AN ILLUSTRATED TIMELINE

By Mark Purdy and Jeff Suess
Foreword by Steve Young

REEDY PRESS

Reedy Press
PO Box 5131
St. Louis, MO 63139, USA
www.reedypress.com

Library of Congress Control Number: 2024939239

ISBN: 9781681065571

Front cover photographs: Focus on Sport/Getty Images; Peter Brouillet/Getty Images; Joseph Patronite/Getty Images; Christian Petersen/Getty Images; Ezra Shaw/Getty Images.

Back cover photographs: Thearon W. Henderson/Getty Images; David Madison/Getty Images.

All images courtesy Getty Images unless otherwise noted.
Cover and Interior design by Crag Gartner. Production by Linda Eckels.

Printed in the United States of America.
24 25 26 27 28   5 4 3 2

CONTENTS

Foreword by Steve Young vii

Introduction ix

Chapter 1
The Adventure Begins — 1946–1958 1

Chapter 2
Growing Pains — 1959–1979 21

Chapter 3
Dynasty — 1980–1990 39

Chapter 4
Finding New Footing — 1991–1998 81

Chapter 5
The Gold, the Bad, and the Ugly — 1999–2016 105

Chapter 6
The Quest for Six — 2017– 131

Endnotes 157

Index 161

Acknowledgments 165

Jerry Rice speeds past San Diego Chargers defenders for a touchdown in Super Bowl XXIX, January 1995.

COURTESY OF AFP VIA GETTY IMAGES

FOREWORD

by Steve Young

When I arrived in the Bay Area from Tampa Bay in 1987, I will admit that I didn't know much about San Francisco 49ers history. I knew that John Brodie had played quarterback for them, but it felt like that was a long time ago, a different world from the team I was joining at Candlestick Park.

I gained far more appreciation for that world when I would see Y. A. Tittle or Frankie Albert at different events and they'd talk about the old days. After I was elected to the Pro Football Hall of Fame, I really got to know the team's other Hall of Famers and loved hearing their stories. I also got a sense for how the team's present was connected to the past from fans who would tell me about Kezar Stadium and what section they sat in, or how birds would poop on them during games, or the favorite players they loved.

It's because of those fans that I feel like the 49ers have become sort of a lifeblood of the Bay Area. The Giants and Warriors have had great success in baseball and basketball. But I watch how 49er fans travel to away games. They're multi-generational and have followed the team for decades, with the same expectations that are so high and the disappointments that are so immense if the expectations aren't fulfilled. That multi-generational feeling, going back almost 80 years, is what puts the 49ers in a different category from the other Bay Area pro teams. This book covers the whole timeline.

For the last 45 years since Bill Walsh became our head coach, those expectations have been the same, right? It's been to win the Super Bowl. And if that doesn't happen, whose fault is it? I'm quite familiar with that dynamic. But from my perspective, it was a thrill to be part of a revolution in football. It wasn't just Bill's offense and coaching methods being so far ahead of what everybody else was doing. It was Eddie DeBartolo saying: "I'm not just an owner, I'm a partner with the players." The way he took care of us, the way he was there with us and alongside us, all of that was a foreign concept back in the 1980s. But over time, other teams adopted it and I think the NFL is thriving today because of it.

Being so together from top to bottom of the organization, feeling that way, also made you play a certain way. It led directly to our success. As long as the franchise holds on to that philosophy and builds on it, the future is always going to be bright for the team. I think the epitome of that is Kyle Shanahan, who has expanded on what Bill did, and how John Lynch and ownership deals with the players. I'm glad that when I retired from the playing field, I decided to stay and raise our family in the Bay Area. I get to watch it all up close.

—Steve Young, June 2024

George Kittle and Christian McCaffrey celebrate a touchdown during the 2023 season.
COURTESY OF COOPER NEILL/GETTY IMAGES

INTRODUCTION

Santa Clara University in the 1920s, with the lawn where Tony Morabito and Al Ruffo met and dreamed of a San Francisco football team.
COURTESY OF SANTA CLARA UNIVERSITY LIBRARY

In the beginning, there was a game of catch on the Santa Clara University campus.

The year was 1928. Tony Morabito, looking to blow off steam after class, headed off to the grassy main quad with a football—a puffy lump of leather back then—and quickly spotted Al Ruffo. The two scholars shook hands and introduced themselves. As they tossed the ball back and forth, they struck up a conversation. The topic wasn't quantum mechanics. It was blocking. And tackling. And the sport that obsessed them.

That conversation ignited the idea that became the San Francisco 49ers, the Bay Area's most popular and successful professional sports team.

Decades later, a 92-year-old Ruffo sat in the living room of his San Jose home and remembered the tripwire moment when Morabito's vision coalesced. It was a little like listening to Wilbur Wright describe the moment that Orville brought up the idea of building a glider. By 1944, Morabito was a successful lumber businessman in San Francisco. Ruffo, a law school grad, was his legal counsel.

"Tony walked into our company office one day," Ruffo said, "and he asked me, 'Al, do you think a professional football team would go around here?' I told him, 'Tony, it's a natural.' And Tony said, 'All right, let's go to work.'"[1]

The book you hold in your hands serves as a timeline of everything that happened next.

It is one hell of a saga, involving unforgettable characters who ate raw meat, invented new offenses, created last-second miracles, and won five Super Bowls.

Northern California likes to think it is too sophisticated and smart to get really excited about something as gauche as sports entertainment that involves grunting and sweating. But not when it comes to the 49ers. From those early beer-soaked bleacher rousers at Kezar Stadium to the current howlers at Levi's Stadium, the entire region has tended to lose its collective mind over the Niners. When the 2023 team was pushing hard for a sixth Lombardi Trophy, that mania was understandable. But as you dive into the team's history, you'll see that it's nothing new.

Tony Morabito's instinct was correct back in 1928 when he went searching for a football friend on the quad. He just didn't realize the entire Bay Area would be ready to play.

John Gonzaga, Frank Morze, and Bruce Bosley of the 49ers block for Hugh McElhenny at Kezar Stadium, 1959.

COURTESY OF ROBERT RIGER/GETTY IMAGES

CHAPTER 1 THE ADVENTURE BEGINS 1946–1958

FOR THE FIRST 12 years of their existence, the San Francisco 49ers played in two different leagues with three head coaches, two star quarterbacks, three playoff games, and far more disappointments than triumphs.

Numerous future Hall of Famers took the field at Kezar Stadium, both as 49ers and as visitors, although this was long before the actual Hall of Fame was founded in Canton, Ohio. Those early pros were just happy to earn a paycheck and not break any bones while surviving to play the next Sunday. Along the way, as they built a franchise foundation, they produced some wild Sunday afternoons and legendary performances.

Many of those games took place in a home stadium that was often half full but was still one of the rowdiest and most daunting venues in the country. That part of the story began in 1925. >>>

1925

Mary Kezar's Stadium Is a Gift to Golden Gate Park

The 49ers and Green Bay Packers at Kezar Stadium, 1962
COURTESY OF MARTIN JACOBS

AS FAR as anyone knows, Mary A. Kezar was not a football fan when she died in 1922. But she was a Golden Gate Park fan. Her will bequeathed the city of San Francisco a $100,000 gift to build a memorial in the park to honor her mother and cousins, who were early California pioneers during the gold rush. (Yes, original 49ers.)

The will's executors decided that a 25,000-seat sports stadium (later expanded to 59,000) would be exactly what Mary wanted. Civic officials tossed in another $200,000. Kezar Memorial Stadium, designed by architect Willis Polk and shoehorned into the park's cramped southeast corner, ceremonially opened on May 2, 1925.

Almost immediately, the first ceremonial seagull dropped the first ceremonial seagull deposit on the place, amidst the persistent fog.

No one ever called Kezar Stadium a gorgeous venue. The weather was often misty and inhospitable. The cement infrastructure, dark tunnels, and wooden bleachers were spartan to the max. So were the scarce restrooms. Only 18,000 seats were located between the goal lines.

Kezar showcased track meets, motor racing, rugby, even boxing matches. But the top regular attractions were high school and college football games. There was almost no parking, so fans hopped onto bus lines or hiked through the park to reach the stadium gates.

Gene Washington, the 49ers wide receiver who played two seasons at Kezar, didn't hate it. "It was a throwback," Washington said. "You were in a neighborhood, between Golden Gate Park and a bunch of houses. It had a real homey feeling to it. Nothing like the big, huge stadiums with the big, huge parking lots that came after."[2]

Tony Morabito's Dream Quest Succeeds

AS TONY MORABITO sat in his office at the lumber transport business he had founded, something else occupied his mind. Took up daily residence there, really.

Football. Football. And more football. Also, football.

Morabito had been consumed by the game while growing up in a sports-loving Italian American family. A high school halfback, he was undersized for the next level and lasted only one season at Santa Clara University. But he followed the Broncos as an adult, attending their frequently sold-out games on Sundays at Kezar Stadium, where St. Mary's and the University of SanFrancisco also drew large crowds.

During the war years, however, those programs were suspended. Morabito was not in uniform because of his bad hearing. Those vacant football Sundays in the city amplified Morabito's notion of starting up a pro team. He directed his attorney pal from college, Al Ruffo, to draw up the proper paperwork and game plan. In the spring of 1944, they went to Chicago with a $25,000 check to see NFL commissioner Elmer Layden about purchasing an expansion franchise.

Layden basically dismissed them as naïve hicks from the outback. He asked semi-sarcastically where San Francisco was in relation to Los Angeles, mocked their mission and questioned their credentials.

"He talked as if California was some kind of foreign country," Ruffo said years later. "Layden told us, 'You gentlemen had better go out and get a football first, then come back and see me.'"[3]

The All-American Football Conference owners, 1948

COURTESY OF BETTMANN ARCHIVES VIA GETTY IMAGES

Peeved and embarrassed, Morabito walked down the street and called on Arch Ward, the *Chicago Tribune* sports editor who was organizing a new league. On June 4, 1944, Morabito and prospective owners from New York, Cleveland, and four other cities solidified their agreement as the All-America Football Conference (AAFC). They announced that their first season would be in 1946 if the war was over by then.

49ers founder Tony Morabito

PRESS RELEASE

It was. Morabito had his dream franchise. One of his business partners, Allen Sorrell, came up with the new team's nickname, honoring the gold-rush pioneers who had spawned the modern San Francisco. Now all the newly born 49ers needed were players and a coach.

Buck Shaw Comes Aboard

THERE WAS no real shock when Tony Morabito hired Buck Shaw as the 49ers' first head coach in 1945. Shaw was the Santa Clara head coach, admired and accomplished. He'd guided the Broncos to Sugar Bowl victories in 1937 and 1938—both times over Louisiana State University, even then a Southern powerhouse.

As a bonus, Shaw was the coach from central casting when it came to impressing potential 49ers ticket-buyers. At age 46, he was tall and still solidly built, with gleaming white swept-back hair that earned him the nickname "the Silver Fox." He had played tackle at Notre Dame, where he was coached by Knute Rockne and absorbed Rockne's strategies. Most importantly, the Silver Fox was very available in 1945. Santa Clara had suspended football so that its players could go fight. Shaw eagerly signed up for Morabito's new venture. There was no actual 49ers team to coach in 1945 as they waited for the war to end. Morabito allowed Shaw to spend that season nearby in Berkeley, where Cal had not suspended sports. The Bears went 4–5–1. Shaw then turned his attention to building the 49ers roster from scratch for the 1946 opener.

The players he and Morabito signed soon learned that Shaw was no screaming taskmaster. He was a bond and securities salesman in his off hours. He took a respectful and brainy approach to motivating his men.

"He wasn't very vocal and never raised his voice," quarterback Frankie Albert said years later. "He was so low-key. Sometimes during practice when we'd be playing poorly, he'd say, 'Your minds aren't on the game today. Take a couple of laps and go in.' And as we'd take our laps, some of us would get together and say, 'Let's stay out another 20 minutes or so.'"[4]

The extra practice would pay off in those first few AAFC seasons.

The 49ers' head coach Buck Shaw, right, confers with Norm Standlee and Frankie Albert.
COURTESY OF BETTMANN ARCHIVES VIA GETTY IMAGES

Anybody Want to Play?

BUCK SHAW had to assemble the first 49ers team without a draft or free agency. Who was around and beefy? Who was not signed to an NFL team but good enough to play in the AAFC? Who was serving in Japan and might want to play pro football when he returned home?

Ken Casanega fit the bill. A decorated Navy bomber pilot and a pre-war halfback at Santa Clara, he had not played football in five years. In Okinawa, after completing his last mission, he received a contract offer from Shaw, his college coach. Casanega signed the deal, returned stateside ("I went up to Lake Tahoe and ran around those hills for two weeks to get in shape"[5]), and would go on to lead the AAFC in punt returns. Casanega's resume was typical. Of the original 34 players on the first San Francisco 49ers roster, 30 were war veterans.

Shaw also used the quality of local talent to his advantage. He signed quarterback Frankie Albert, fullback Norm "Chief" Standlee, and guard Bruno Banducci from Stanford, where they had an been part of an undefeated 1940 season. End Alyn Beals and guard Visco Grgich came from Santa Clara. The players' average salary was $4,500.

Albert was the highest paid at $10,000. The left-hander was not your typical quarterback, even for that time. At 5-foot-9, he was not physically imposing. But he was the most deceptive weapon in the sport. At Stanford, he had mastered the T formation quarterback position, tutored by coach Clark Shaughnessy, the formation's father and guru. Albert usually called his own plays or simply made them up on the spot. His ballhandling misdirection skills—especially his "naked" bootleg runs around end after faking to a running back—caused fits for opposing defenses. "Frankie Albert was like a riverboat gambler," future teammate Joe Perry described him. "He had a sharp mind and did the unexpected."[6]

He could pass as well. Albert threw for an AAFC record 88 touchdowns in the four seasons the league existed.[7] His favorite receiver was Beals, a touchdown machine with 46 scores in that four-year span. In the days of leather helmets and two-way players, the passing game was still developing.

"Buck Shaw was a great innovator," Beals said. ". . . He was one of the first coaches to start spreading the ends out. We used to have the ends spread only about a foot. He kept spreading them off the tackles a little at a time. It opened up the passing game."[8]

COURTESY OF TRANSCENDENTAL GRAPHICS/GETTY IMAGES

September 8, 1946

Kickoff at Kezar

FINALLY, THERE was football. The 49ers flew to Southern California in late August for the first of two exhibition games. They defeated the Los Angeles Dons 17–7 before a sparse crowd of 8,000 at Balboa Park in San Diego. A week later, on September 1, nearly 40,000 curious football fans witnessed the 49ers' 34–14 triumph over the Chicago Rockets at Kezar Stadium. Press reports pointedly noted that a thick fog swirled across the field.

After that, the real thing. The New York Yankees came to Kezar on September 8 for the season opener. Frankie Albert was ready with some trickery. The first touchdown in franchise history ensued. Albert dumped a quick 6-yard pass to fullback Johnny Strzykalski, who lateraled the ball to halfback Len Eshmont for a 62-yard dash to the end zone. It was the most exciting moment in a downbeat 21–7 loss to New York before 35,698 spectators and some 25,000 empty seats. Even fewer fans showed up the next week for a 21–14 victory over the Miami Seahawks and for the following Sunday's 32–13 win over the Brooklyn Dodgers.

However, in the five-game road trip that followed, the 49ers built a reputation as must-see entertainment. They put on offensive shows that culminated with a 34–20 defeat of Cleveland in the Browns' first loss ever, as the 70,386 fans at Municipal Stadium watched Albert outdazzle the brilliant Otto Graham. Home crowds picked up after that. The 49ers concluded the season with a 9–5 record and finished second in their division to the Browns.

AAFC WESTERN DIVISION 1946-1949

CHICAGO ROCKETS
CLEVELAND BROWNS
LOS ANGELES DONS
SAN FRANCISCO 49ERS

The 49ers hit quarterback Otto Graham, handing the Cleveland Browns their first-ever loss in 1946.
COURTESY OF BETTMANN ARCHIVES VIA GETTY IMAGES

Morabito was nevertheless happy. He claimed a loss of about $150,000 for the season, which he said was acceptable. He hadn't counted on a profit. Alyn Beals led the AAFC with 10 TD catches. The 49ers also had the league's top rushing offense. They were creating a positive buzz. Morabito sensed the future was sunny, despite the Kezar fog.

Joe the Jet Breaks a Barrier

TO SELL tickets, teams need stars. Tony Morabito knew Joe Perry could be a star. The trouble was, Perry ran almost too fast. Often in practice, a quarterback would take the snap from center, pivot to hand off the ball and . . . oops. Perry wasn't there. He was already through the offensive line. Frankie Albert said Perry reminded him of the airplanes flying overhead and began calling him "Joe the Jet."

Tony Morabito loved it. The team owner was not a consistently lovable personality. But he had a consistent open heart and mind in terms of racial issues. At a time when both the NFL and AAFC were overwhelmingly white from goalpost to goalpost, Morabito rejected that norm. In 1947, he signed the first player of Japanese ancestry to a pro football contract. Kaname "Wally" Yonamine of Hawaii, a running back, played one season for the 49ers before switching sports to baseball. That opened the door to Morabito's even bolder decision to sign the 49ers' first Black player.

Perry was that man. After serving in the Pacific during the war, Perry played for the Alameda Naval Air Station football team outside Oakland. A tip sent Morabito across the Bay for a look. The 6-foot, 207-pound Perry was dominant—and after his discharge, immediately hired.

In his 1948 rookie season, Perry averaged 7.3 yards per carry and scored 11 touchdowns—as a backup fullback, not a starter. In 1949, coach Buck Shaw wisely sent starter Norm Standlee to the defensive side of the ball. Perry led the AAFC in rushing—and in absorbing cheap shots. At the bottom of piles, Perry's eyes were poked and his groin punched by opponents who hated his skin color.

"It was rough as hell," Perry said. "Lots of things were said on the field. You can imagine what they were. It was probably worse playing football instead of baseball, like Jackie Robinson did, because football is such a physical game. The 49ers were great, though. If one person was in a fight, the whole team was in a fight. We were like a big family."[9]

The biggest blowback Morabito received to Perry's signing came from his unenlightened AAFC partners. Morabito told the story of watching a home game alongside Buffalo Bills owner Jim Breuil.

Photos from a 1948 49ers game program.
COURTESY OF AUTHOR'S COLLECTION

"It makes it tough on all of us who don't sign a Negro," Breuil said. "Why did you do it, Tony?"

Just then, Perry broke off a 58-yard TD run as the Kezar crowd roared.

Morabito turned to Breuil and said: "That's why, Jim."[10]

Niners halfback Len Eshmont, playing defense, takes off downfield after intercepting a New York Yankees pass in 1949.
COURTESY OF BETTMANN ARCHIVES VIA GETTY IMAGES

The Great Brown Wall of Cleveland

IN *MOBY-DICK*, Captain Ahab had his nemesis the Great White Whale. In the AAFC, the 49ers had the Great Brown Brick Wall. The Niners kept slamming into it. And never did scale it.

In the 1948 season, the 49ers put on a dazzling show for their fans. Frankie Albert threw 29 TD passes. Alyn Beals caught 14 of them. The team averaged 35.4 points per game and entered early November with a 10–0 record. And then, brick wall. Two games in three weeks against the Browns.

In Cleveland before a record pro football crowd of 82,768, Albert completed just six of 15 passes for 32 yards. The 49ers lost a grind-it-out decision 14–7. Fourteen days later back at Kezar Stadium, 61,000 customers showed up for the rematch. They witnessed fireworks. Albert threw for three touchdowns. The 49ers put up 28 points. The Browns put up 31. Second place. Again.

A year later, the 49ers vowed things would be different. On October 9, the Browns came to Kezar riding a 29-game unbeaten streak. And for one magnificent Sunday, the 49ers vanquished all their demons. Albert had five TD passes. Joe Perry rushed for 155 yards. The Niners won 56–28. It was the franchise's first true signature victory.

"On this day, the 49ers were the greatest football team I've ever seen," said retired 78-year-old coaching icon Pop Warner, who was watching from the press box.[11] The sight didn't last. In ensuing weeks, the 49ers lost another Cleveland shootout 30–28. With no AAFC divisions that season, four of the seven teams qualified for the playoffs. The 49ers beat the New York Yankees in the semifinals before flying to snowy, sloppy Cleveland for the championship game. Browns 21, Niners 7. Of course.

"Definitely, they were stronger," Perry said of the frustrating rivalry. "Cleveland hurt us . . . but we hurt ourselves more. We'd average 35 points and some teams would outscore us."[12]

Coach Paul Brown and the Cleveland Browns dominated the AAFC, winning the 1949 championship over the 49ers.

COURTESY OF BETTMANN ARCHIVES VIA GETTY IMAGES

Fullback Joe Perry churns out yards against the Los Angeles Rams, the 49ers' new NFL in-state rivals.
COURTESY OF ROBERT RIGER/GETTY IMAGES

NFL WESTERN CONFERENCE 1950–1966

- BALTIMORE COLTS
- CHICAGO BEARS
- DETROIT LIONS
- GREEN BAY PACKERS
- LOS ANGELES RAMS
- SAN FRANCISCO 49ERS

1950

Merging with the Big Guys

THE NFL was not always a colossus blotting out the sun. In mid-20th-century America, pro football played fifth fiddle to college football, Major League Baseball, boxing, and horse racing. Radio and television coverage was spotty, varying from market to market.

Things began to change around 1950, right about when the AAFC merged with the NFL. Only three AAFC franchises joined up with the older league—Cleveland, San Francisco, and Baltimore. The additions signaled that the NFL was serious about going coast to coast.

But in 1950, the 49ers weren't thinking about the big picture. They were thinking about the big guys—the Chicago Bears, Philadelphia Eagles, and other NFL juggernauts. Tony Morabito just wanted to fit in and be competitive. The 1949 season had produced a small profit for him. Yet his original financial partners, Allen Sorrell and Ernie Turre, were so unsure of the team's future that they exited. Tony's brother, Vic, stepped in to pick up the financial slack.

The Morabitos soon discovered how far behind the curve they were. Their AAFC roster was not NFL ready. Paul Brown in Cleveland had stocked up on depth and strength for the new challenge, bursting from the gate with a victory over the defending champion Eagles as a springboard to an NFL title. The 49ers did not retool. Some of their linemen were outweighed by 30 pounds in their new league. In the first preseason game, the Washington Redskins rolled over the San Francisco weaklings 31–12.

"Frankly, they did not look capable of beating any team in the National Football League," wrote *San Francisco Chronicle* sports editor Bill Leiser the next day.[13]

"Organizational-wise, the NFL was way ahead," halfback Sam Cathcart said. "The Chicago Bears would have 10 coaches; we had three. We were like a college team, still, in that era."[14]

The 49ers lost their first five games and went on to finish 3–9, sixth in their seven-team division. The Morabitos got the memo. They needed better players, more star attractions, and tougher men.

Leo the Lion

FOR THEIR first NFL draft choice, the 49ers could not select a large wild animal. As an alternative, they picked Leo Nomellini, known as "Leo the Lion" during his college days. Nomellini logged a record 147 consecutive games over 14 seasons with the 49ers. He played on both the offensive and defensive lines, earning All-Pro honors at both positions. For six years, 1951 through 1955, he played every down of every game on both sides of the ball. He once scored a touchdown by blocking a punt and chasing down the ball 30 yards into the end zone.

"I really like to play football," Nomellini said, in an understatement. "It's tough and it's hard and no pro football owners can pay a player enough for the punishment they take. You just have to like it—and I do."[15] At 6-foot-3 and 257 pounds, the Lion would not be considered big by modern standards. In the 1950s, his sculpted physique was awe-inspiring. Born in Italy before immigrating with his parents to Chicago when Mussolini took power, Nomellini never played high school football. He learned the sport on a Marine Corps team during World War II. Following VJ Day, he enrolled at the University of Minnesota and became a two-time All American.

For the 49ers, it was a no-brainer to bring him aboard as they sought to beef up for their new life in the NFL. The Lion spent his first three seasons as an offensive tackle, for which Joe Perry was grateful. He joked that Nomellini could knock someone back 20 feet with a friendly slap on the back.

"He was so strong, so strong," said Dan Colcicho, who played alongside Nomellini as a defensive end. "The thing around the league was, 'Don't get him mad.'"[16]

Given the NFL salary scale of 1950, players needed offseason jobs. Nomellini leveraged his outgoing personality to join the pro wrestling circuit—and made more money than he did sacking quarterbacks. Nomellini held the region's tag-team championship with partner Hombre Montana and drew 12,000 to the Cow Palace when he faced heavyweight champ Lou Thesz. The Lion pinned Thesz but—go figure—lost the match on a disqualification technicality. The 49ers ignored that blemish on Nomellini's record when they retired his No. 73 jersey.

COURTESY OF DIAMOND IMAGES/GETTY IMAGES

Lineman Leo "The Lion" Nomellini moonlighted as a pro wrestler, on the left, throwing champ Lou Thesz in a 1955 match.

COURTESY OF BETTMANN ARCHIVES VIA GETTY IMAGES

Million Dollar Sundays

THE 49ERS had football's most famous foursome in the 1950s. "The Million Dollar Backfield" was among the greatest to play the game, with the absolute best nickname. To set the record straight, they never made close to a million dollars, singularly or as a unit. So where did the moniker come from? Branding. Hype. And necessity.

As the 49ers fought to gain NFL credibility, it became apparent that maximum offensive weaponry was needed. Joe Perry was not enough.

When Baltimore's franchise folded in 1951, the 49ers picked up the team's quarterback, Y. A. Tittle. He had a stronger arm than Frankie Albert, but the two split time at the position, triggering the team's first quarterback controversy. Halfback Hugh McElhenny, the 49ers' top pick in 1952, was one of the best open-field runners in the game. He averaged 7.0 yards a carry and was named Rookie of the Year. Then, for the 1954 season, the 49ers signed bruising runner John Henry Johnson out of the Canadian League. This combination was perfect for the full-house T formation that coach Buck Shaw used, with three running backs on the field on every play.

Dan McGuire, the 49ers public relations man, came up with "The Million Dollar Backfield" label for the quartet—not for their paychecks, but for the rich thrills they would provide for fans.

Hugh McElhenny COURTESY OF ROY H. WILLIAMS/*OAKLAND TRIBUNE*/MEDIANEWS GROUP VIA GETTY IMAGES

McGuire wasn't wrong. Each of the four had distinct skills that meshed perfectly in Shaw's offensive vision. Perry was the north-south speed merchant. McElhenny, nicknamed "The King," could smoothly glide before making cuts sharper than the fancy tailored suits he wore off the field. Johnson was a wrecking ball who bulldozed holes open for the other two if he wasn't carrying the ball himself.

Tittle orchestrated it all, calling plays in the huddle. He spread around carries so well that Perry, McElhenny, and Johnson all finished among the NFL's top eight rushers in 1954, combining for 2,245 yards and 23 touchdowns.

For three seasons, from 1954 to 1956, the team's Million Dollar Sundays were can't-

Y. A. Tittle COURTESY OF HULTON ARCHIVE/GETTY IMAGES

miss attractions at Kezar and on local television. Unfortunately, the won–loss record failed to match the offensive highlights. Defense mattered, too. And the 49ers went 16–18–2 over that stretch. "That was one hell of a backfield," said McElhenny. "Even with all that talent, we could never quite win it."[17]

History has been kind to Perry, Tittle, McElhenny, and Johnson. They are the only four-man backfield to all earn Pro Football Hall of Fame induction. How much were they actually paid? Niners historian Dave Newhouse estimates that the foursome's combined salaries added up to roughly $70,000 a season. Or about $930,000 less than a million.

John Henry Johnson COURTESY OF BUCK JOSEPH/ *OAKLAND TRIBUNE*/MEDIANEWS GROUP VIA GETTY IMAGES
Joe Perry COURTESY OF LONNIE WILSON/*OAKLAND TRIBUNE*/MEDIANEWS GROUP VIA GETTY IMAGES

The 49ers face the Browns at Kezar Stadium, 1956.
COURTESY OF HY PESKIN/GETTY IMAGES

The 6-foot-9 Bob St. Clair (79) loomed over Joe Arenas (22), Bob Toneff (74), and other 49ers on their sideline in a game against Cleveland at Kezar Stadium, 1956.
COURTESY OF HY PESKIN/GETTY IMAGES

Goodbye, Buck– Welcome Back, Frankie

IN 1954, the 49ers were banged up, having lost Hugh McElhenny and other key players for the season. Yet they were still in the playoff race. But in a "must-win" game against the Detroit Lions, the Niners were mauled, losing 48–7. Critics savaged 49ers coach Buck Shaw, saying it was the same old story: the team started fast, then folded when it counted.

Tony Morabito thought his team had first-place talent. After a third-place finish, he fired Shaw, saying: "I think the record should have been better and the championship could have been won, despite the injuries."[18] It was time to try something new.

The 49er players were not in unanimous agreement. "Frankly, I don't know how they are going to find a better man than Buck," said receiver Gordy Soltau.[19]

League officials must have nodded. They tabbed the ousted Shaw to coach the West squad in the postseason Pro Bowl. When his team won, with 49ers Billy Wilson and John Henry Johnson playing major roles, the West squad's players presented Buck the game ball.

Shaw went on to coach the last place Philadelphia Eagles in 1958 and after two turnaround seasons won the 1960 NFL title. Then he retired on top.

Meanwhile, the Morabitos hired former 49ers assistant Red Strader as their next head coach. Wrong move. Unlike his predecessor, Strader was a rabid disciplinarian. He even refused to let players drink water on the practice field. After a 4–8 season of bad vibes that included a five-game losing streak, Strader was also fired.

Morabito's next step was a stunner. He convinced his favorite retired quarterback, Frankie Albert, to replace Strader. Albert's total coaching experience consisted of one year as a 49ers assistant. But he felt he owed it to the Morabitos to accept their offer. Albert's unpredictable temperament—he had well-known swings of wild energy and morose despair—made his hiring a big risk. But the next few years produced the 49ers' only playoff team of the 1950s and games that people still talk about seven decades later.

San Francisco head coach Buck Shaw and fullback Joe Perry after Shaw's last game as coach in 1954

COURTESY OF BILL YOUNG/*SAN FRANCISCO CHRONICLE* VIA GETTY IMAGES

1957

Tittle and Owens and "Alley-Oop"

COURTESY OF SAN FRANCISCO 49ERS

AS quarterback, Frankie Albert had been a master of spontaneous creativity. But when he took over as the team's head coach in 1956, he insisted on calling all the plays from the sideline. Quarterback Y. A. Tittle hated the idea. Tittle had a much more potent arm and an ability to stand in the pocket and deliver rocket balls while absorbing punishment if necessary. Tittle thought he'd earned the right to dictate his own calls like other NFL quarterbacks. He and Albert were friends. But they kept arguing about the issue.

Tittle eventually won the argument—partly by coming up with his own improvisational piece of genius, assisted by rookie receiver R. C. Owens. On October 6, 1957, Tittle sent his teammate to an end zone corner and lofted a pass that the 6-foot-3 Owens jumped up and caught over a shorter Los Angeles Rams defender for a touchdown. Tittle and Owens did this twice in the 23–20 upset win.

"R.C. was a college basketball player so it was like going up for a rebound for him," Tittle explained. "After the game, he told me, 'I can do that every time.'"[20]

So they did. More or less. Mostly more. Tittle dubbed it the "Alley-Oop" play, based on the name of a popular comic strip, which in turn took its title from the French phrase *allez hop!* shouted by acrobats about to jump. Owens was no comic character or French acrobat. But he did know how to time his impressive end zone leaps to levitate over just about any defensive back.

The "Alley-Oop" worked again for a last-minute winning touchdown in a 35–28 victory over Detroit for the division lead. It worked over and over, adding to the 49ers' passing game options, which included productive ends Gordy Soltau and Billy Wilson. Tittle wound up completing 63.1% of his passes for 2,157 yards and 13 touchdowns that season and was named NFL Player of the Year by the United Press.

As for Owens? He acquired the nickname of "Oop," which he proudly embraced the rest of his life. Today, a variation of the same play is called a "fade." But whenever and wherever it is thrown, the spirit of "Oop" lives.

San Francisco 49ers head coach Frankie Albert gives a play to receiver Gordy Soltau, 1956.

COURTESY OF MEDIANEWS GROUP/*OAKLAND TRIBUNE* VIA GETTY IMAGES

San Francisco 49ers quarterback Y. A. Tittle launches a pass over Los Angeles Rams defenders.
COURTESY OF ROBERT RIGER/GETTY IMAGES

A Heart Gives Out and the 49ers Rise Up

IT IS telling that the 49ers' two most memorable games of the 1950s both involved heartbreaks. One of the heartbreaks was far more tragic than the other.

Tony Morabito, the man who founded and owned the 49ers, was not a healthy man. He had an iffy cardiovascular system. Morabito's doctors, knowing full well how his emotions rose and fell during 49ers games, told him he should sell his football team to avoid a bad outcome.

Morabito declined. If he was going to die, he said, it might as well be at a 49ers game. On October 27, 1957, his horrible wish came true. Just before halftime at Kezar Stadium, with the Chicago Bears holding a 17–7 lead, Morabito collapsed in his booth. A priest was summoned to issue last rites. An ambulance arrived, but Tony Morabito was already gone, at age 47.

The players in the halftime locker room heard of their owner's collapse. When they returned to the sidelines for the third quarter, they were told Morabito had not survived.

On October 30, 1960, the team placed a memorial bench at Kezar Stadium in Tony Morabito's honor.

COURTESY OF BOB CAMPBELL/*SAN FRANCISCO CHRONICLE* VIA GETTY IMAGES

"There was a moment of stunned silence, then the bench became a madhouse of crying, shouting players," team publicist Dan McGuire remembered.[21]

The reaction morphed into fierce football in the second half. Leo Nomellini, his eyes weeping, hit Chicago quarterback Ed Brown hard enough for the ball to pop out. It was scooped up by 49er teammate Bill Herchman, who motored 46 yards to the goal line. After another interception, Y. A. Tittle hit Billy Wilson on an 11-yard scoring pass. Niners 21, Bears 17.

"That was the battle cry unsaid: 'C'mon, let's win this one for Tony,'" Tittle said. "It gave us that little extra adrenaline."[22]

Morabito literally loved the 49ers to death. For one afternoon, they paid back his love as best they could with a tear-stained second-half comeback. The next heartbreak would arrive soon enough.

Playoff Cheers Are Canceled

THE ROLLER coaster 1957 season led to a sweet 49ers reward: Their first NFL postseason game, their only playoff appearance of the 1950s—and, as it turned out, the 1960s as well.

Indeed, if there was a watershed moment when the 49ers gained their top-shelf status in the cultural kitchen of San Francisco and the Bay Area, it took place in the buildup to that December day when the Detroit Lions visited Kezar Stadium.

Events of the previous four months, stirring and sad, had finally done it. Local college football, previously the top Northern California gate attraction, was now in second place. There was only minor league baseball and no NBA basketball. The 49ers were it. They had created a major buzz with their "Alley-Oop" passes, a five-game winning streak, and Tony Morabito's emotional passing. The long-awaited playoff game on December 22, 1957, was televised across Northern California. Detroit and San Francisco, tied for first place in the West, were playing for the right to face Cleveland for the NFL title.

"We had split with the Lions during the year," 49er tackle Bob St. Clair remembered. "We were very confident about winning. We came out smoking."[23]

And how. The 49ers rolled out to a 24–7 halftime lead. Lions players claimed they could hear the 49ers players prematurely celebrating on the other side of their locker room wall. Kezar's public address announcer was explaining when tickets for the championship game would go on sale.

Euphoria increased early in the third quarter when a field goal built the 49ers' lead to 27–7. Detroit then replaced quarterback Bobby Lane with Tobin Rote, who caught a break.

"All our defensive backs got hurt," St. Clair said. "We had to put a running back, J. D. Smith, back there. He didn't know how to play the position. Rote had a field day."[24]

Niners receiver Billy Wilson snags a touchdown pass over defender Jack Christiansen in the 1957 playoff game against the Detroit Lions.
COURTESY OF BETTMANN ARCHIVES VIA GETTY IMAGES

Y. A. Tittle had the opposite, throwing three interceptions. The Lions scored 24 straight points to win 31–27. The capacity Kezar crowd went silent. One attendee was future 49ers head coach George Seifert, a student at Polytechnic High School across the street. Seifert was a stadium usher on Sundays. He vividly remembered riding the bus back to his house that night and palpably sensing the gloom that permeated the city. It would take a long time for the 49ers franchise to totally erase that postseason ignominy.

John Brodie quarterbacked the 49ers from 1957 to 1973, through lean times as well as two NFC Championship Games.

COURTESY OF FOCUS ON SPORT/GETTY IMAGES

CHAPTER 2 GROWING PAINS 1959–1979

THE SIXTIES AND Seventies were colorful decades for the 49ers. And that doesn't even include the tie-dyed Summer of Love in Golden Gate Park outside Kezar Stadium—which preceded yet another Autumn of Not So Groovy Football inside the stadium. The 1967 season's mediocre 7–7 record was typical of the era.

In truth, what made that 49er time period so colorful was the cast of characters, both before and after the team moved to its new home field at Candlestick Park in 1971. San Francisco's rosters included a lineman who ate uncooked steaks, a linebacker known as "The Intimidator," an MVP quarterback, and a halfback who came out as the NFL's first openly gay player after his retirement. If reality television had existed back then, several players' shows could have set ratings records.

To be sure, the 49ers were good enough from 1970 to 1972 to make the playoffs and meet up in colorful contests with the Dallas Cowboys. All three times, the 49ers lost, launching a classic NFL rivalry. Painful years? Yes. Maddening years? Yes. But never boring. The colorful growing pains set the table for glory years to come. >>>

Bang! It's the Shotgun

RED HICKEY became the 49ers' head coach in 1959 when Frankie Albert, stressed out by the job, resigned after another pedestrian 6–6 season. Hickey had been Albert's top assistant. He promised to rev up the offense. Amidst middling football, Hickey drew up a big bang.

In November 1960, the 49ers faced the Baltimore Colts, the two-time defending NFL champions. The Colts had a fierce pass rush. Hickey countered by having quarterback John Brodie stand six yards behind the line of scrimmage. Running backs and receivers spread out wide. Linemen took larger splits. Hickey's logic was that with Brodie deeper in the backfield, Baltimore's defenders would have a harder time reaching him. Brodie would also have more time to scan the defense before deciding where to go with the ball. The new scheme led the Niners to a 30–22 upset victory.

Reporters asked Hickey what he called his newfangled invention. He said it was "spread right and spread left," based on an old formation Pop Warner had drawn up in the 1930s. The journalists were disappointed. They coaxed the 49ers coach to provide a sexier name.

"Well, I'm an old country boy," drawled Hickey, who'd grown up in rural Arkansas. "I used to go hunting with a shotgun. Why don't we call it the 'shotgun'?"[25]

The big bang helped the 49ers win four of their last five games and finish 7–5. They just missed the playoffs. Success continued in 1961—for a while. The 49ers blew out the Lions 49–0 using a "triple-barreled shotgun"[26] that rotated a different quarterback on every down. But the Chicago Bears soon figured out the shotgun's flaw. They overloaded the middle of their defensive line and stormed unblocked through the widely split 49er linemen to discombobulate John Brodie. The Niners were humiliated 31–0. Just like that, as quickly as it had exploded, the shotgun was blunted.

Quarterback John Brodie follows guard Bruce Bosley on a scramble against the Cleveland Browns in 1961.
COURTESY OF DIAMOND IMAGES/GETTY IMAGES

Hickey Fizzles in Non-Sizzling Sixties

THE BEARS' undoing of the shotgun was a disaster for Red Hickey, who had pinned all his hopes on the formation in 1961. Y. A. Tittle, who was never comfortable in the "gun," was traded to the New York Giants (who he quarterbacked to three straight championship games). Billy Kilmer was brought in to share QB duties with Brodie. Then Hickey exposed Hugh McElhenny to the NFL expansion draft. The new Minnesota Vikings quickly claimed him. Hickey also traded franchise icon Joe Perry to the Colts and dealt veteran linebacker Ed Henke to the Cardinals.

None of this thrilled Hickey's remaining troops. The 49er locker room atmosphere was sour and gurgling. Hickey didn't care. He seemed to enjoy screaming at players and staff members. "He tore that team apart," receiver Gordy Soltau said.[27]

After forsaking the shotgun, Hickey used a pro-set offense the rest of 1961. Brodie approved. He threw three TD passes in a 41–31 rematch victory over the Bears. The Niners won three of their last five games. R. C. Owens had a career season, becoming the first 49er receiver to reach 1,000 yards. But thanks to the shotgun misfire in the early part of the schedule, the team's 7–6–1 record meant fifth place.

Things were no better (6–8) the following year, and 1963 was even worse. Before the season, Brodie and Kilmer were in separate car accidents. Hickey quit after the first three games, all losses. Players celebrated. But still didn't win. Assistant coach Jack Christiansen took over. He presided over a 2–12 stink bomb of a final record. The rest of the Sixties smelled slightly better, but basically followed the same "meh" script.

The worst moment occurred when Vic Morabito, who had succeeded brother Tony in the owner's office, died of a heart attack on May 10,

PETER BREINING/*SAN FRANCISCO CHRONICLE* VIA GETTY IMAGES

The Morabito widows, Jane (left) and Josephine, took ownership of the 49ers after the deaths of their husbands.
JOHN O'HARA/SAN *FRANCISCO CHRONICLE* VIA GETTY IMAGES)

1964. The Morabito widows, Jane and Josephine, inherited the team. They were pioneers as the rare female owners of a pro sports franchise. The widows appointed Lou Spadia, an original 49er employee, as general manager and team president. Although the 49ers weren't winning many games, they were respectable under "the Morabito ladies," as the press called them. "They had a special kind of style and it was nice," wrote *San Francisco Examiner* columnist Wells Twombly.[28]

Meanwhile, in 1975, Dallas coach Tom Landry resurrected and refined the shotgun offense to wild success. The formation should have sued Red Hickey for abandonment.

Roland Lakes (60) and Charlie Krueger (70) hold off the Chicago Bears in a muddy 1969 game at Kezar Stadium.

COURTESY OF FOCUS ON SPORT/GETTY IMAGES

Hall of Fame Trio

Cornerback Jimmy Johnson returns an interception against the St. Louis Cardinals, 1974.

COURTESY OF MICHAEL ZAGARIS/GETTY IMAGES

WHEN PEOPLE bought tickets for a 49ers game in the mid-1960s, they had to put up with a lot. Clammy fog. Scarce parking outside Kezar Stadium. Choppy, sloppy turf. Drunks in the bleachers. Strong odds of a fistfight in any row.

Fans did enjoy one benefit. They could watch three future Hall of Famers in home uniforms. All three were big personalities.

Bob St. Clair, the biggest of the big at 6-foot-9 and 263 pounds, owned the most San Francisco DNA of any 49er, ever. As a kid, he roamed the city's Ingleside neighborhood. Then he became an All-City lineman at Polytechnic High across the street from Kezar Stadium. This earned him a football scholarship at the University of San Francisco. The Dons played at Kezar, too.

Eleven seasons as a 49er only amplified St. Clair's legend. His long limbs specialized in vicious leg-whip blocks—legal in those days—and forearm violence. He could also initiate off-the-field scraps. Once, while driving home from Kezar after a loss, he stopped the car to shut up some sidewalk hecklers with his fists.

But the large man's calling card was his affection for raw meat. Infamously, he would order uncooked restaurant steaks on the road. Or once, raw liver at a team dinner.

"The waiter set it down in front of me, with a small side of blood," St. Clair said in his memoir. "I immediately started slicing it up and eating it. The veterans on the team started laughing. They were used to it. But some of the rookies made a quick exit. So did the woman at the next table."[29]

49ers linebacker Dave Wilcox

COURTESY OF MICHAEL ZAGARIS/GETTY IMAGES

Defensive terror Dave Wilcox was even more violent than blood-loving Bob. Rams quarterback Roman Gabriel praised Wilcox, saying he played outside linebacker "like Dick Butkus plays middle linebacker."[30] A seven-time Pro Bowler, Wilcox was nicknamed "The Intimidator" for the collisions he perpetrated without mercy or apology. "It wasn't like he'd get a big hit every now and then," said teammate Jimmy Johnson. "The big hits were a thing of regularity."[31]

Johnson committed his own All-Pro excellence. After two seasons as a receiver, he transitioned into a shutdown cornerback so effective that opponents began throwing the ball elsewhere. Yet over 213 games, he accumulated 47 interceptions. Johnson was still playing cornerback at age 38, and in his final game he allowed just one reception for nine yards.

How the 49ers Helped Launch NFL Films

THE NFL surged past other sports in popularity during the 1960s for many reasons. Television network exposure topped the list. But a close second was the birth of NFL Films, which brought artistry to the league's highlights with slow motion, sideline closeups, and dramatic narration over stirring music to transform games into epic spectacles.

Because of NFL Films, pro football was suddenly as cool as it was brutal. The league couldn't have devised a better tool to spread the gospel to potential new fans. And the 49ers were in the gospel mix right from the start—though not always as the winning team. Two examples are still featured wherever NFL Films are unspooled.

On October 25, 1964, the 49ers lost 27–22 to the Minnesota Vikings at Kezar Stadium. No one remembers that final score. What they remember is how, in the fourth quarter, Vikings defensive lineman Jim Marshall ran the wrong way with a fumble recovery for 66 yards to the 49ers' end zone and scored two points for them on a safety.

"I didn't know what was going on," said the 49ers' Charlie Kreuger, trailing the play.[32]

Neither did Marshall. His blunder occurred when the 49ers' Billy Kilmer lost the ball as Marshall chased him downfield from behind. Marshall scooped it up without breaking stride, saw an open field and a goalpost, sprinted to the end zone and tossed the ball in the air to (mistakenly) celebrate. The NFL Films crew captured it all.

A year later, the 49ers had an entire afternoon of bad moments thanks to Chicago rookie running back Gale Sayers. In a muddy 61–20 rout at Wrigley Field, Sayers scored six touchdowns, tying an NFL record that still stands.

What made the feat unforgettably cinematic was Sayers' variety show. For his first touchdown, he took a short pass and weaved through multiple 49ers on an 82-yard play. He sprinted 50 yards for the next one, then rushed for three more TDs before capping off his day with an 85-yard punt return for six points. The NFL Films footage turned Sayers into a superhero.

Marshall's goof and Sayers's masterpiece unquestionably set off NFL Films' 1960s ascension. The 49ers were supporting characters. They still helped make league history.

Gale Sayers' career day against the 49ers made him a superhero on NFL Films.

COURTESY OF BETTMANN ARCHIVES VIA GETTY IMAGES

An NFL Films cameraman catches the action.

COURTESY OF OTTO GREULE JR./GETTY IMAGES

Uncommon Men in a Groovy Time

THE INTERSECTION of Haight and Ashbury in San Francisco was just a six-block walk from Kezar Stadium. From 1965 to 1970, when the 49ers left the neighborhood, walking those six blocks on Sunday afternoons was, like, you know, a real trip, man. Psychedelic longhairs freely mixed with beer-swilling crew cuts on the way to Golden Gate Park, where football and marijuana were both hot attractions.

There were no reports of culture clashes. San Francisco is that sort of place. The city seems to breed uncommon tolerance and uncommon people. The 49ers of those years were no exception.

Defensive lineman Charlie Krueger was a perfect example. After a broken arm nixed any action his rookie year, Krueger played 15 seasons in San Francisco, missing only eight games. His fundamental fierceness was the basis for his nickname of the "Textbook Tackle"—although Krueger probably should have skipped more plays. Instead, he endured regular painkilling shots. Later, he discovered that 49er doctors had misled him about knee injuries that left him in constant pain as an older man. In 1981, Krueger became the first former NFL player to successfully sue his team for damages, to the tune of $2.3 million.

Dave Parks, by contrast, was an extremely brief and bright star. The top pick in the 1964 NFL draft, Parks took the 49ers' tight end play to another level. In 1965, he scored on passes of 83, 80, and 79 yards while leading the NFL in catches (80) and receiving yards (1,344). The following year, his 66 catches were third in the league. In 1967 he held out for five games in a salary dispute, then left in 1968 as a free agent to New Orleans.

There was also running back Dave Kopay. He gained fame in another way. In 1975, three years after his last NFL game, Kopay became the first athlete in a major North American sport to come out as gay. He joined the 49ers in 1964 and led the team in rushing. Over his four years with the team, he also built a reputation as a smashmouth special teams player. When Kopay announced his sexual orientation, his former teammates generally respected his willingness to be himself.

"After Kopay revealed he was gay," said Charlie Krueger, "he thanked me for the decency I'd shown him. I believe in individual rights."[33] No wonder he thrived for 15 seasons in San Francisco.

Defensive tackle Charlie Krueger was a mainstay with the 49ers in the 1960s.
COURTESY OF FOCUS ON SPORT/GETTY IMAGES

Kezar Stadium's proximity to San Francisco's Haight-Ashbury area meant it drew an interesting crowd.
COURTESY OF *SAN FRANCISCO CHRONICLE* VIA GETTY IMAGES

Head coach Dick Nolan elevated the level of the 49ers' play, reaching the playoffs three years straight in the 1970s.

COURTESY OF JAMES FLORES/GETTY IMAGES

NFC WEST DIVISION 1970-1994
ATLANTA FALCONS
LOS ANGELES RAMS
NEW ORLEANS SAINTS
SAN FRANCISCO 49ERS

1968

Dick Nolan, a New Sheriff in Town

AFTER TOO many years of vexing football and dwindling Kezar Stadium crowds, general manager Lou Spadia had seen enough. In December 1967, Spadia sacked head coach Jack Christiansen, who had won only 26 of the 67 games he'd coached. Certain players had told Spadia that Christiansen was too mellow a guy to be an NFL head coach. The goal was to replace him with someone less easygoing. Spadia raided the Dallas Cowboys to find the new sheriff.

Dick Nolan was his name. As an NFL player, he had been a hard-tackling defensive back before serving as Dallas coach Tom Landry's top defensive assistant. The 49ers had forever been criticized for having a fireworks offense with a dud defense. Nolan, handsome and steely eyed, seemed the perfect matinee-idol solution.

For the next five seasons in San Francisco, he often was. The 49ers won three division titles and made their first playoff appearances since 1957 in front of packed houses at Kezar. Nolan was hard driving but not unreasonable, according to the men who played for him.

"He was a class act, the kind of guy who stood by his word," said tackle Len Rohde. "He was straightforward and fair."[34]

Well, there was one dissenting voice: Quarterback John Brodie, who loathed the way Nolan rotated his quarterbacks, seemingly on a whim. "A crummy guy," Brodie called him.[35] Yet paradoxically, Brodie had his best seasons under the no-nonsense sheriff and almost reached the Super Bowl.

As the first head coach to raise legitimate championship hopes for San Francisco fans, Nolan more than deserved a merit badge.

1970

John Brodie's Peak Year

NO QUARTERBACK of the 49ers had a more torturous career than John Brodie. Through his 17 seasons with the team, playing for four different coaches, he constantly had to fight for playing time as he won, lost, and then re-won battles for the starting job.

Along the way, Brodie also broke his arm in a car wreck, endured shoulder cortisone injections, and suffered knee injuries. He kept his helmet jammed on as he exited the field after games as protection against beer cans and garbage tossed by angry fans.

He persevered through the garbage. The 49ers made the playoffs zero times between 1958 and 1969. The customers wanted to take it out on somebody, and Brodie was the most visible somebody. He told writers that he understood the fans' frustration but was annoyed that the team didn't employ a quarterbacks coach, saying: "I had not learned how to play quarterback and I'd been there for eight years. I'd just get by on my natural ability and I could throw the ball and I could move around laterally. So, that was the way it worked."[36] Y. A. Tittle was hired to coach the offensive backfield in 1965, and things started to click for Brodie. Three times Brodie led the NFL in pass completions and passing yardage.

For one magical season in 1970, all the junk melted away. The 49ers' front office surrounded him with his best cast of blockers and receivers, allowing him to manifest the full Brodie. He led the league in completions, passing yardage, touchdowns, and total offense while being sacked just eight times. He was named league MVP.

"Forget about the statistics," said wide receiver Gene Washington, who snarfed up more than one third of Brodie's 2,941 passing yards that season. "He was truly one of the great, great football players."[37]

Coming down the stretch, the 49ers needed to win their final three games to clinch a division championship. Brodie led comeback victories in all three. After the last, writers asked him to speculate about a possible Super Bowl run.

"Let me savor this one first," Brodie said. "It took 13 years to get it. This is my first title since my high school days at Oakland Tech. I've got to find a place tonight to celebrate."[38]

Quarterback John Brodie had a career year in 1970 and was named the league MVP.
COURTESY OF RUSS REED/*SPORTING NEWS* VIA GETTY IMAGES

Finally, a Playoff "W"

THE NFL'S decision to expand and merge its 16 franchises with the American Football League's 10 teams ended up being a boon for the 49ers. It meant six divisions, not two. Beginning in 1970, to win a division title and a guaranteed playoff spot, Dick Nolan's team merely needed to finish ahead of three other teams. The 49ers were placed in the NFC West with the Atlanta Falcons, New Orleans Saints, and Los Angeles Rams.

This made little sense geographically. But it made 49ers fans incredibly happy when their team stormed out of the merger starting gate with a 10–3–1 record. And finished first. And went to the playoffs. And upset Minnesota in the first playoff game—on the Vikings' home field in sub-zero wind-chill weather, no less. Bruce Gossett, the 49ers placekicker, wore thermal socks to keep his toes warm. But after San Francisco's 17–14 victory, he said the cold hadn't bothered him.

"I was thinking about the $30,000 reward for winning the ballgame," Gossett said. "Whenever you think about that much money, you're going to keep warm."[39]

Brodie threw for one score and ran for another—while playing in a short-sleeved jersey. Meanwhile, the 49ers defense managed the Vikings even better, causing four turnovers. Minnesota didn't score an offensive touchdown until one second remained in the game. The Vikings' other TD came on a fumble return. The 49ers at long last owned an NFL playoff victory.

When the Niners' charter flight home landed, thousands showed up at the San Francisco airport chanting: "Beat Dallas!" The Cowboys were coming to Kezar for the NFC Championship Game and were four-point underdogs. The winner was bound for Super Bowl V.

That wouldn't be the 49ers. The defensive struggle was tied 3–3 at halftime. In the third quarter, Brodie threw two interceptions to set up Dallas touchdowns. He shook that off to hit Dick Witcher for a 26-yard score that cut the Cowboys' lead to 17–10. But that's how the game ended, in the last NFL game played at Kezar before the team moved to Candlestick Park. Dallas had foiled the 49ers. That same sad Cowboys song would be stuck on repeat for years to come.

Tight end Ted Kwalick catches a pass against the Minnesota Vikings in the 1970 divisional game. The 49ers finally won their first NFL playoff game.

COURTESY OF FOCUS ON SPORT/GETTY IMAGES

October 10, 1971

Moving to the Stick

LONG BEFORE the 1970s, team president Lou Spadia and the Morabito widows realized that Kezar Stadium would not be the 49ers' forever home. The old hunk of concrete, with its splintered bleacher seats and hazardous restrooms, was unfit for the top-tier sports attraction that the NFL was becoming.

Since 1960, the San Francisco Giants had been playing major league baseball at Candlestick Park on the southern fringe of the city in a venue best known for its howling cold weather. But the Stick was "modern" for its era, with individual chair-back seats, escalators, and wide concourses. In 1969, the San Francisco Board of Supervisors proposed a $14 million expansion to accommodate football—although the sightlines still favored baseball—and to increase seating capacity from 42,000 to 61,000. The 49ers signed up.

The 49ers moved into Candlestick Park in 1971. The much-maligned stadium saw the team's biggest success.
COURTESY OF DAVID MADISON/GETTY IMAGES

Cynics said that the supervisors took a bad baseball park and spent millions to transform it into a worse multi-sport venue. Yet Candlestick was an upgrade from Kezar. Plus, San Francisco autumn weather is always warmer than summer weather. And the team was coming off an NFC Championship Game appearance. The forecast was for an exciting new 49ers era in a packed stadium.

The first regular season game, on October 10, 1971, against the Rams, was witnessed by 44,000 spectators and 17,000 empty seats. The 49ers lost 20–13. Oh, well.

Happily, better days were ahead for the Niners at their new home, including 27 playoff games and eight NFC title games.

For the first eight years the 49ers played at the Stick, players had to deal with the wretched new phenomenon of artificial turf, which was installed so that the playing surface could handle both baseball and football. The plastic grass, laid down on an asphalt base with virtually no padding, drew less than rave reviews. "We called it Candlestone," said 49ers defensive end Cedrick Hardman. Defensive tackle Bill Sandifer sarcastically complimented the surface for being "a great parking lot to play on."[40]

Fans, who didn't have to suit up, adjusted better. The vast parking lots surrounding Candlestick made for formidable tailgating. And the 49ers carried on their tradition of the "Christopher Milk Section" free-seats-for-kids program at Kezar with Candlestick's "Junior 49er Minor Club" sponsored by Berkeley Farms Dairy. Now, the team just needed to serve up some championship cookies with all that milk.

Fans had given the 49ers a rough time over the years, but shout out "Well done!" to the players after they beat the Washington Redskins in a 1971 playoff game.

COURTESY OF BILL YOUNG/*SAN FRANCISCO CHRONICLE* VIA GETTY IMAGES

Not Doing Dallas

THE COWBOYS. The damn Cowboys. Again. And again.

The 1970 through 1972 seasons were by most measures a party-bus ride for the 49ers. It was the best three-year stretch in franchise history to that point. There were stirring regular-season comebacks. Three NFC West division titles. Three playoff appearances. Playoff game victories over Minnesota and Washington.

But the party ride always ended when the Dallas Cowboys stepped off their own bus to break up the festivities. All three seasons, the Cowboys ended the Niners' aspirations to reach a Super Bowl, in ever more soul-crushing fashion.

First came the postseason defeat at Kezar after the 1970 season. Then another NFC title game loss the following year in Texas. Finally, the 1972 schedule concluded with an agonizing playoff loss at Candlestick Park. It's odd how history carves patterns. In the 1940s, the Cleveland Browns kept blocking the 49ers' championship path. The Kansas City Chiefs would do the same thing in the 21st century. But in the 1970s, the Cowboys were the immovable objects.

Dallas's featured attraction of the era was its Doomsday Defense. In the 1971 NFC Championship defeat, the Cowboys held San Francisco to a mere field goal and intercepted John Brodie three times in a 14–3 decision.

The 49ers finally cracked the Doomsday code in the 1972 divisional playoff and scored 28 points. Fullback Larry Schreiber ran for three touchdowns. Brodie, having lost his starting job to Steve Spurrier before winning it back late in the season, steered the Niners to a 15-point lead after three quarters.

Unfortunately, football has four quarters. Cowboys quarterback Roger Staubach came off the bench and threw two TD passes in the final 90 seconds, sandwiched around an onside-kick recovery when the 49ers' Preston Riley had the ball bounce through his hands. Dallas 30, San Francisco 28.

"I've never gotten over it," Riley said more than 40 years after his muff. "It has haunted me every day of my life."[41]

"We were that close," said teammate Len Rohde.[42]

The 49ers would eventually and ultimately conquer their Dallas demons. But it would take another decade to do so.

John Brodie had a rough time against Dallas defensive tackle Bob Lilly. The 49ers fell to the Cowboys in the playoffs three years in a row in the 1970s.

COURTESY OF FOCUS ON SPORT/GETTY IMAGES

Sad-Face Seventies

IF YOU want to smile while reading, skip this page. After the ugly 1972 playoff collapse against Dallas, the 49ers football platter fell off the table and shattered into pieces. Dick Nolan, so successful at building up the team to title-contending standards, lost the plot. Over the next three seasons the Niners went a combined 16–26 as a consequence of bad decisions, bad luck, and bad draft choices.

John Brodie was sick of it. The quarterback announced that 1973 would be his last season after Nolan gave the starting job to Steve Spurrier. The coach let Brodie start the last game of the season against Pittsburgh as a farewell to the Bay, but an arm injury limited his playing time to barely more than a quarter. He completed six passes for 79 yards, zero touchdowns, and two interceptions, including a pick-six. It was an unfair end to an illustrious career. But Brodie was smart to exit.

Because the following year was sadder still. Star kick returner Vic Washington had a public shouting match with Nolan in training camp and was traded, as were other disgruntled veterans. The 49ers lost seven of their first nine games as Nolan used five different quarterbacks en route to a 6–8 record. From 1973 onward, a dank misty gloom settled over Candlestick.

Sunshine occasionally broke through. The 49ers had many sublime Sunday moments with talented players. Gene Washington was a gliding marvel at wide receiver. Running back Delvin Williams gained 1,203 yards in 1976. Ted Kwalick was a rock-hard rock star at tight end.

Those three just couldn't do it all. After the Niners finished up another 5–9 season in 1975, Nolan was fired. Monte Clark was hired three weeks later. A tough former 49ers lineman with an upbeat personality, Clark traded away Spurrier and acquired quarterback Jim Plunkett from New England. Plunkett no longer flashed the Heisman Trophy magic he'd shown at Stanford, but he created positive energy as the 49ers improved to 8–6 overall in 1976.

It would be the team's last winning record of the decade. The Morabito widows sold the franchise before the 1977 season and sad faces returned in force, with a revolving door of three more short-term losing coaches. But the sale of the franchise would soon change the team's image forever. If you have read this far, you can start smiling again.

Quarterback Jim Plunkett had a miserable time in San Francisco but went on to win two Super Bowls with the Oakland Raiders.

COURTESY OF MICHAEL ZAGARIS/ GETTY IMAGES

Youngstown Comes to San Francisco

IN 1977, Josephine and Jane Morabito sold the football team that they had inherited from their late husbands to the DeBartolo family of Youngstown, Ohio. However, the deal took a twisted path to fruition. When the Morabito widows decided to offload the 49ers, their attorney tapped an unlikely source for help: Al Davis, owner of the Oakland Raiders across the Bay, who knew NFL politics better than anyone.

The football-loving DeBartolos—with a fortune built by Edward DeBartolo Sr.'s self-made rise as the country's top shopping mall developer—had initially found their entry point into the league thanks to Joe Thomas, who had grown up near Youngstown before becoming an NFL executive in Miami and Baltimore. Thomas had befriended DeBartolo Sr. and promised that Davis could help secure the 49er franchise for the DeBartolo family.

The 49ers' new owner, Eddie DeBartolo Jr., center, made early missteps such as signing worn-out running back O. J. Simpson, left, and hiring coach Pete McCulley, right.
COURTESY OF BETTMANN ARCHIVES VIA GETTY IMAGES

It all came together in March 1977. The DeBartolos bought 90 percent of the 49ers for $17.5 million. Davis pocketed a $100,000 finder's fee. The league forbade corporations from acquiring teams, so Edward DeBartolo Sr.'s son, Eddie, was named the owner of record. Naively, Eddie walked through the 49ers front door and face planted. He hired Thomas as general manager, demoting the popular Lou Spadia. Thomas was a disaster waiting to happen. He happened immediately.

Thomas, who had been fired from several previous jobs, justified his reputation as an egomaniac know-it-all blowhard. He ripped down photos of former 49er greats at the team offices and tossed memorabilia and record books into the trash, saying the team's "history starts today." Eddie DeBartolo didn't know any better and sided with Thomas on all matters. Monte Clark was fired as head coach after refusing to give up control of player personnel. Clark was replaced by Ken Meyer, who was canned after going 5–9 and replaced by Pete McCulley, who was dumped after starting 1-8 in 1978, and replaced by Fred O'Connor to finish up a 2–14 season before he was fired, too. Did you keep track of all that?

In fairness, all of those coaches had been saddled with dreadful rosters, headed up by an on-his-last-legs O. J. Simpson, whom the 49ers obtained from Buffalo in exchange for five 49er draft picks. It was another terrible Thomas move. "Joe Thomas was to football franchises what scorched earth is to landscaping," said offensive lineman Randy Cross.[43]

Eddie DeBartolo would soon wise up and re-landscape.

Bill Walsh Changes Everything

EDDIE DEBARTOLO was in a quandary. For two years he watched general manager Joe Thomas run the 49ers into the ground before too many empty seats at Candlestick Park. Eddie's decision to dismiss Thomas was the easy part. The hard part was figuring out who to hire next. Barely 32 years old, DeBartolo was the league's youngest owner. He had no network of experienced football people to call for advice or recommendations.

What he had was Ron Barr. As a local television sportscaster, Barr had developed a friendly relationship with DeBartolo. Barr also produced the weekly *Stanford Football Highlights* show that featured the university's head coach, Bill Walsh.

Bill Walsh, noted for his cerebral approach to football, was known as "the Genius." He certainly transformed the 49ers into perennial Super Bowl contenders.
COURTESY OF FOCUS ON SPORT/GETTY IMAGES

Over dinner late in 1978, Barr told DeBartolo he should hire Walsh to coach and rebuild the 49ers. Eddie DeBartolo did not know much about Bill Walsh, despite his successful bowl teams at Stanford.

DeBartolo was not even familiar with Walsh's first NFL coaching experience in Ohio, where he'd spent eight years as Paul Brown's top offensive assistant with the Cincinnati Bengals. There, Brown and Walsh had concocted a new method of playing football—using the pass to set up the run, rather than vice versa, with short throws that were essentially long handoffs. They figured out how to transform modestly talented quarterbacks like Sam Wyche and Virgil Carter into true NFL offensive weapons, thanks to the X's and O's of what came to be known as the "West Coast Offense."

DeBartolo took Barr's suggestion and set up a meeting with Walsh in a suite at the San Francisco Fairmont Hotel. Later, Eddie would say that 10 minutes into their conversation, he'd already decided to hire Walsh. "I just knew that he was the guy," DeBartolo said.[44]

Walsh used the leverage of the 49ers' current horrible state to make one demand: He would be in total control of football operations, reporting only to DeBartolo. Eddie agreed and gave Walsh a contract for $160,000 a year, more than twice the average NFL player's salary at the time. It was a lot of money. But in retrospect, a bargain for the man who would change everything.

"The Cincinnati offense started playing advanced checkers with my offensive designs," Walsh said later. "By the time I got to San Francisco, I was teaching teams how to play advanced chess."[45] But first, he needed the game pieces.

The Best Third-Round Pick Ever

JUST FOUR months after taking the 49ers' job, Bill Walsh had to conduct his first-ever NFL draft as a head coach. He couldn't blow it. But the team did not even have a first-round selection. Joe Thomas had traded away that pick as part of the O. J. Simpson deal.

Luckily, Walsh was able to make the best third-round draft pick in league history.

You will find many people, from NFL "insiders" to hotel valets, who take credit for bringing Joe Montana to Walsh's attention. Tony Razzano, the 49ers scouting director, probably has the best claim. His analysis had Montana ranked higher than any other quarterback in the draft, though members of Razzano's staff strongly disagreed. They thought Montana, despite his winning heroics with Notre Dame that included an epic comeback in the 1979 Cotton Bowl while suffering from the flu, was too inconsistent and too slight at 6-foot-2 and 185 pounds.

Sam Wyche, Walsh's new hire as the 49ers' quarterbacks coach, also deserves credit for ignoring those scouts. Wyche had organized a workout in Southern California with Montana throwing the ball to James Owens, a UCLA running back who would become the 49ers' second round pick. Days before the draft, Wyche convinced Walsh to join him in Los Angeles for a second evaluation session. On the return flight to the Bay, Walsh told Wyche that if Montana was still available in the third round, he would be the 49ers' pick.

"People said he didn't have a strong arm but he threw the ball fine," Walsh would say later. "He was quick, agile, and fluid in his movements, almost like a ballet dancer."[46]

And so, with the 82nd selection of the draft, Montana's name was called. He had a good preseason but, save a few cameo appearances, sat on the bench as a rookie behind starter Steve DeBerg. Montana finished the season with 13 completed passes and one touchdown. But watching DeBerg operate Walsh's system in 1979 wasn't the worst training. Even though the 49ers won only two games, they had the NFC's top-ranked pass offense. Nine of their losses were by 10 points or less.

Progress was apparent. With the decade of the Seventies mercifully over, the man in the No. 16 jersey would make sure that the Eighties unspooled more joyfully.

Quarterback Joe Montana was noted for his comebacks at Notre Dame and led the Fighting Irish to a national championship.

COURTESY OF BETTMANN ARCHIVES VIA GETTY IMAGES

Head coach Bill Walsh and quarterback Joe Montana were brilliant together, orchestrating an offense that dominated the NFL in the 1980s.

COURTESY OF FOCUS ON SPORT/ GETTY IMAGES

CHAPTER 3 DYNASTY 1980–1990

WHEN THE 1980s began, the 49ers were just another NFL team. By the end of the Eighties, they were a dynasty. They were no longer prospectors. They were fully fledged gold miners.

If anybody says they saw it coming, they are lying. Bill Walsh had never overseen an NFL roster. The quarterback was a skinny risk. The defense had too many unproven rookies. The 1970s had been dominated by the Pittsburgh Steelers, a muscle team that hammered opponents into the ground. The 49ers were more of a clever board game, violent when necessary but more eager to keep opponents off balance and guessing.

The Team of the Decade got off to a slow start with a 6–10 record in 1980 before rocketing to a startling Super Bowl season in 1981 that built to another title in 1984 by the franchise's best ever team. After intriguing ups-and-downs, there were two back-to-back championships as the team transitioned from Walsh to his successor, George Seifert. With classic games and future Hall of Famers galore, it was a blast to watch. Fasten your seat belt and enjoy the next 40 pages. >>>

Behold the Future

FOR THE first three months of the decade, The Team of the Eighties failed to wow people. Instead, the 49ers were The Team of Oh-No-Here-We-Go-Again. A three-game winning streak in September raised hopes before an eight-game losing streak dashed them. Bill Walsh kept giving fans whiplash as he rotated the starting quarterback job between Steve DeBerg and Joe Montana.

But that was before one monumental Sunday in December when the future rose up and slapped the league in the face, capturing the entire country's attention.

On December 7, 1980, at Candlestick Park, the 49ers and their 5–8 record were facing the pitiful New Orleans Saints, who were 0–13. The Niners were favored, big. The 37,949 loyalists who showed up were amped. That is, until Saints quarterback Archie Manning threw three TD passes before the 49ers even made a first down. New Orleans sprinted to a 35–7 halftime lead, with the 49ers' only TD coming on a punt return by Freddie Solomon.

In the locker room at halftime, Walsh didn't froth at the mouth or berate. He sarcastically told his players that he didn't want to embarrass them because they were handling that quite well on their own. He did, however, utter these fateful words: "In the next 30 minutes, you're going to learn a lot about yourselves."[47]

Whereupon the 49ers went out and learned that they could author the greatest regular season comeback in NFL history to that point.

Montana, starting for the third straight week, began by engineering an 88-yard drive that concluded with his own 1-yard TD run. He followed it up with a 71-yard TD pass to Dwight Clark. Two more scoring drives in the fourth quarter, set up by two New Orleans fumbles, tied the score at 35–35 at the end of regulation. The crowd was pleased.

After the 49ers stopped the Saints on their first overtime possession, Montana moved the offense in position for Ray Wersching to kick a game-winning 36-yard field goal.

Niners 38, Saints 35. Montana's second-half magic made waves nationally. More significantly, it electrified his fellow workers. "This was the game where his teammates learned to believe in him," Walsh said years later. "Modern 49ers history started there."[48]

Joe Montana proved to be the right quarterback fit for Bill Walsh's new offense.
COURTESY OF FOCUS ON SPORT/GETTY IMAGES

Dwight Clark Rises with the Changing Tide

FOREVER AND always, the fall of 1981 will be the most beloved six months of 49ers football for the fans who witnessed it. The first time is the best. That autumn was the best. The 49ers surprised people week by week as they won game after game, rising from years of mediocrity, misery, and almosts to go 13–3 in the regular season and win a Super Bowl.

Rising along with them was a tall drink of happy wide-receiving attitude named Dwight Clark. He was a 49er not necessarily by accident but certainly by good fortune. Before the 1979 draft, Bill Walsh traveled to Clemson University to check out quarterback Steve Fuller as a potential top pick. Walsh called Fuller's apartment but instead reached his roommate, Clark, who was on his way out the door to play golf. Walsh asked Clark if he'd mind coming along to catch Fuller's passes at the workout. Clark was no great shakes. He'd only caught 11 passes his senior season at Clemson.

As it turned out, Fuller didn't excite the 49er head coach—but Clark did, because of his size (6-foot-4, 215 pounds), hands (excellent) and footwork (underrated). San Francisco drafted him in the 10th round. Clark's affable personality connected well with fellow rookie Joe Montana. They also connected on the practice field, developing chemistry through hard work after the official sessions were done.

"I didn't have a clue about reading defenses, making adjustments," Clark said. "A lot of times, I'd run a 10-yard hook and if the guy was inside me, I'd kind of push off and run a breakout. Joe could read that."[49]

Their reading homework reached complete fruition in 1981, as Montana became the undisputed starter. Every Sunday he and Clark seemed to create the top highlight. A statement romp by 31 points over Dallas featured a 78-yard TD pass to Clark. Against the Rams, a Clark catch-and-run TD covered 41 yards. A signature win at Pittsburgh showcased seven Clark receptions. At Cincinnati, he caught a key 20-yard TD pass in a 21–3 victory. He finished the regular season with 85 catches for 1,105 yards.

But Clark's most awesome and historic catch was still ahead of him.

Wide receiver Dwight Clark became a favorite target for Joe Montana.
COURTESY OF RONALD C. MODRA/GETTY IMAGES

Ronnie Lott was the driving force behind the 49ers' hard-hitting defense in the 1980s.
COURTESY OF DAVID MADISON/GETTY IMAGES

Lott Arrives with a Boom (and a "Woo!")

THE BIGGEST myth about the 49ers of the 1980s is that their offense, curated by Bill Walsh, was light years ahead of the rest of the NFL and flattened everything in its path. The truth was 180 degrees different. The offense was indeed a beautiful weapon. But the flattening was done by the 49ers defense, which deserved equal or more credit for the team's success. The center of gravity for that defense was Ronnie Lott.

The team's first-round pick from USC in 1981, Lott made the 49ers' starting lineup as a rookie cornerback. He could not only blanket receivers. He could storm the line of scrimmage to stop runs. His biggest hits—the ones he called his "Woo!" hits—were meant to send messages.

Lott also picked off a passel of passes, including three he returned for touchdowns as a rookie, en route to 63 career interceptions. He was a respected locker room voice and conscience. But the collisions were his best business practice. "I want it to come from my toes, all the way up through my soul," he said. "I want everything to go into my hit."[50]

He had company. Bill Walsh chose three defensive backs in the first three rounds of the 1981 draft, including cornerback Eric Wright and safety Carlton Williamson. The strategy was met with puzzlement around the league. But Walsh knew where his team needed help most. The three rookies, along with veteran Dwight Hicks, made up the starting defensive backfield, dubbed "Dwight Hicks and His Hot Licks."

All four reached the Pro Bowl during their careers. Lott would climb to an even higher tier than the rest. He was named All-Pro as a rookie and five more times after that. He made 10 Pro Bowls, even as he was moved from cornerback to free safety to strong safety. He was elected to the Hall of Fame in 2000. On lists of all-time best NFL defensive backs, Lott is never not mentioned.

His commitment to the game was legendary. Famously, in 1985 after having his left pinky finger crushed between a helmet and his own shoulder pads, the finger bones splintered and broke through the skin. Lott taped up the digit and kept playing until the 49ers lost in the playoffs, then faced the tough choice of either a bone graft with a long recovery or an amputation of the fingertip that would assure he'd be ready for the next season. Lott went with the amputation. His fingers carry Super Bowl rings instead.

Ronnie Lott, one of three rookies in the 49ers' secondary in 1981, is regarded as one of the greatest defenders in NFL history.

COURTESY OF OWEN C. SHAW/GETTY IMAGES

The defining moment in 49er history: Dwight Clark's fingertip catch helped them win the NFC Championship Game over the Dallas Cowboys, January 10, 1982.

COURTESY OF BETTMANN ARCHIVES VIA GETTY IMAGES

"The Catch" vs. Dallas

ON THE plaza outside Levi's Stadium, two statues immortalize one play, the most important moment from 49ers history. To fans, the sculptures of Joe Montana and Dwight Clark are fine art. On January 10, 1982, the two men connected on a pass with 58 seconds left in the NFC Championship Game to defeat the Dallas Cowboys 28–27 at Candlestick Park. But there was so much more to it than those basic facts.

Dallas was the opponent that had tormented the 49ers for an eternity, going back to those three playoff losses of the 1970s. And for much of that Sunday afternoon, the Cowboys were continuing the tradition. Montana threw three interceptions and lost a fumble, handing Dallas chance after chance in a game that featured seven lead changes.

Late in the fourth quarter, Dallas tight end Doug Cosbie caught a 21-yard TD pass to give the Cowboys a 27–21 lead. The 49ers then took possession on their own 11-yard line with 4:54 remaining. Montana coolly guided the offense to the 6-yard line. Time out. On the sidelines, Bill Walsh told his quarterback to run a standard red-zone play: Sprint Right Option.

There was a backstory to that decision. Back in August, in the training-camp heat, Walsh had asked Montana and Clark to stick around after one practice to work on a variation of the basic play. Normally, it called for Montana to roll out and throw the ball to wide receiver Freddie Solomon on a short down-and-out at the goal line. Walsh outlined an alternate version. He wanted Clark to drive forward to the back of the end zone, then cut left before quickly reversing direction to run across the back of the end zone. Montana was then supposed to send the ball high enough above Clark's head to avoid defenders but low enough for him to make the reception. Over and over, they ran the drill as Walsh watched.

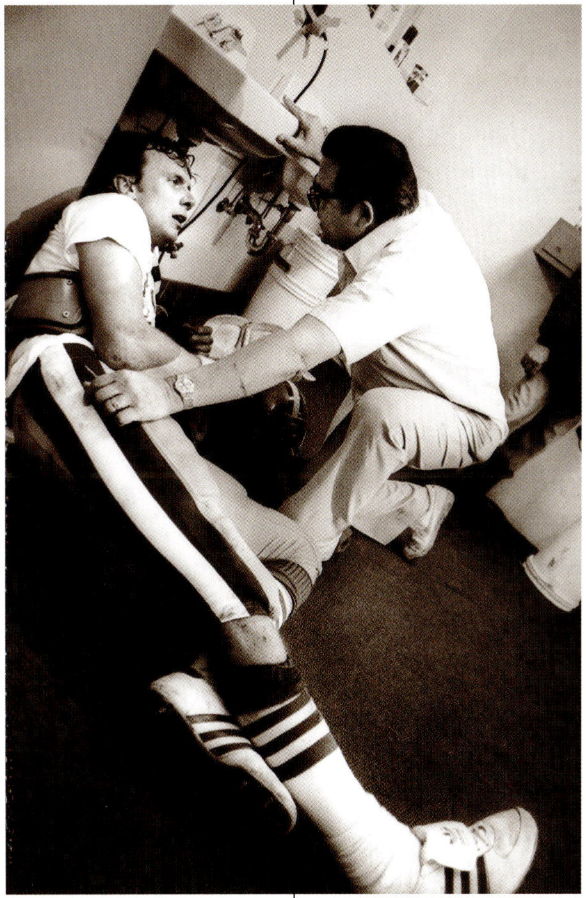

Equipment manager Chico Norton attends to Joe Montana, who collapsed, exhausted, after leading the 49ers offense to victory over the Dallas Cowboys in the NFC Championship Game.
COURTESY OF MICHAEL ZAGARIS

"Until I threw the ball three times an arm's length above Dwight's head, Bill wouldn't let us off the practice field," Montana explained.[51]

Six months later, they executed the play to perfection. Montana rolled right, pumped the ball once to mess with the Dallas pass rushers' timing, then launched the pass that pivoted the franchise's trajectory. Cowboys defensive back Everson Walls could only watch as Clark leaped up to snatch destiny.

"It's a madhouse at Candlestick!" broadcaster Vin Scully orated. "Dwight Clark is 6–4. He stands about 10 feet tall in this crowd's estimation."[52]

"The Catch" set the 49ers on a journey to four Super Bowl titles in the next nine years.

1982

Super Bowl XVI: Hype and Bellhop Bill

BAY AREA citizens were spectacularly unprepared for a 49ers trip to the Super Bowl. Six months earlier, such a thing had been unfathomable. The years since 1946 had been a long slog.

Baffled fans soon rallied. High fives were slapped, often with total strangers. Parties were planned. T-shirts were purchased. A lucky few thousand season ticket holders who'd won a lottery to buy game tickets hurriedly made plans for a trip to the glamorous Super Bowl city of . . . Detroit?

Yes, Detroit. Super Bowl XVI was the first to be staged in a cold climate. Although the game was played indoors in the suburban Pontiac Silverdome, the weather was miserable all week, with ice storms, snow, and bitter breezes.

Bill Walsh flew to Michigan before the team. Seeking to keep his players loose, he paid a bellhop $20 to borrow a uniform and hat, while also donning sunglasses. As the 49ers exited their airport bus, a disguised Walsh kept asking if they needed help with luggage. Finally, a few players caught on to the prank. "They couldn't believe I was dressed as the bellman," Walsh said. "Even when I took my hat off, they still didn't believe it."[53]

It was the start of a zany week. Super Bowl media hype was in full effect as reporters pursued stories about how the 49ers had risen from the depths and made themselves title contenders. Corporate parties, often hosted by automakers, abounded. In blue-collar Pontiac, vacant downtown storefronts were converted to "nightclubs" by placing kegs of beer inside to create a "Bourbon Street North." A few 49ers players, unfamiliar with driving in the snow, skidded their courtesy cars into drifts or ditches and needed tow trucks to extract them.

Bill Walsh in his bellhop disguise at the 49ers' Super Bowl hotel outside Detroit.

COURTESY OF *SPORTING NEWS* VIA GETTY IMAGES

The journey to the Super Bowl had one final glitch on game day. The team took two buses to the Pontiac Silverdome. The first bus arrived fine, with half the roster. The second bus, with the coaches, Joe Montana, and others, became snarled in a traffic jam created by roadblocks for Vice President George H. W. Bush's motorcade.

Minutes ticked by. Nerves jangled. With the bus going nowhere, Bill Walsh picked up the intercom and said no one should worry because the equipment manager was coaching the team, and the 49ers were already ahead by a touchdown. Laughs broke the tension as the bus reached the stadium 90 minutes before kickoff.

The 49ers huddle up during Super Bowl XVI against the Cincinnati Bengals at the Pontiac Silverdome.
COURTESY OF FOCUS ON SPORT/GETTY IMAGES

Earl Cooper celebrates scoring a touchdown against the Cincinnati Bengals during Super Bowl XVI.

COURTESY OF FOCUS ON SPORT/GETTY IMAGES

Super Bowl XVI: Fulfillment and Walsh's Revenge

THE 49ERS' Super Bowl run felt like a fairy tale. But their opponents, the Cincinnati Bengals, had written their own Cinderella story. The Bengals had improved from 6–10 the year before to 12–4 in 1981. They were led by quarterback Ken Anderson, the league MVP, who had learned his trade under Bengals quarterbacks coach Bill Walsh in the mid-1970s.

Walsh had been the presumed successor to Bengals founder Paul Brown when he stepped down as head coach in 1976. But Brown passed over Walsh for the job. Walsh called it a "dramatic disappointment" at the time, but in pre–Super Bowl interviews he said any resentment was gone. Except not really. "Make no mistake, Walsh would have done anything to beat the Bengals," 49ers cornerback Ronnie Lott said. "Although he didn't verbalize his feelings to us, it was obvious that Walsh was obsessed with showing up Brown."[54]

Instead of a fairy tale, the game was a revenge drama.

Act One: The Pounce and Bounce. The 49ers survived fumbling the opening kickoff, thanks to turnovers created by Dwight Hicks and Eric Wright. As they built a 20–0 halftime lead, Walsh pulled out the stops, with a double reverse pass and an unbalanced offensive line that discombobulated Cincinnati's defense. As a capper, he had Ray Wersching squib-bounce his kickoffs on the hard artificial turf, causing two Bengal fumbles.

"I think we just swept them off their feet in the first half," Walsh said after the game. "In the second half, they figured out what we were doing, and you saw we had some difficulty."[55]

Act Two: The Comeback and Pushback. The Bengals rallied to make the score 20–7 and were on the verge of another touchdown at the 3-yard line when the 49ers defense stopped them cold. Two straight times, the Bengals' 249-pound fullback Pete Johnson went nowhere, stuffed by 49ers linebacker Jack "Hacksaw" Reynolds, who had earned his nickname in college by cutting his car in half with that tool. On third down, Anderson tossed the ball to Charles Alexander at the 1-yard line. Niners linebacker Dan Bunz wrestled him sideways and dropped Alexander for no gain. Johnson failed again on fourth down. "I think the goal-line stand broke their back," Bunz said.[56]

Act Three: Holding On and Paying Back. The Bengals scored two more touchdowns, but Montana used up lots of clock time—the 49ers' longest play was a 22-yard pass—to set up Wersching's third and fourth field goals to clinch a 26–21 victory. Rapture ensued in the Silverdome and back in the Bay. And for Walsh, gratification. He had proved a point to his old boss. If it wasn't clear before, there was now no question. The Genius was out of the bottle.

Ronnie Lott leads the cheering after the 49ers stopped the Bengals at the goal line during the third quarter of Super Bowl XVI.
COURTESY OF BETTMANN ARCHIVES VIA GETTY IMAGES

Vexation and Motivation

AFTER THEIR Super Bowl XVI victory, the 49ers endured two seasons of sludge and vexation, which concluded with a controversial playoff loss that ultimately served to ignite a remarkable stretch of excellence.

But first, there was the ugly train wreck of 1982. The 49ers started 0–2, and then the NFL Players Association went on strike for eight weeks. It split the locker room—union militants vs. non-militants—and the tense atmosphere lingered when games resumed. The Niners finished 3–6 in a shortened schedule. After the final game, Bill Walsh candidly identified another factor, one that infested many NFL teams in the anything-goes 1980s. "Drugs were a primary culprit," he said. "Some of our key players didn't show up to play and cocaine was the reason why."[57]

Walsh was so drained by the experience that he skipped the end-of-the-year team meeting. Players were miffed about Walsh's insinuations that they hadn't taken winning seriously in 1982.

The coach had fences to mend, and he vowed to get the team back on track in 1983. Eddie DeBartolo lifted Walsh's profile by naming him team president. He responded by making a trade with the Rams for slippery running back Wendell Tyler, then drafting Roger Craig, a multi-purpose back out of Nebraska. The 49ers managed a 10–6 record and beat Detroit in the first playoff round, setting up the NFC Championship Game against the Washington Redskins.

On mushy turf at RFK Stadium, the 49ers fell behind by three touchdowns but charged back to tie it at 21–21 in the fourth quarter. On the next Washington drive, officials made a questionable pass interference call. A ball sailed high over the head of Redskins receiver Art Monk and was obviously uncatchable, which under NFL rules would mean no flag. (Walsh memorably opined that "a 10-foot Boston Celtic couldn't have caught it."[58]) The penalty set up Washington's winning field goal in a 24–21 decision.

The 49ers swarm Washington Redskins running back John Riggins.
COURTESY OF FOCUS ON SPORT VIA GETTY IMAGES

The 49ers, convinced that the better team had been cheated out of another Super Bowl trip, used the loss as fuel for making sure that 1984 would not end the same way. "It became our biggest motivation, without me even trying to make it so," Walsh said.[59] The rest of the league would become unwitting victims of that motivation.

The Peak of the Peak

WHEN SUMMER training camp opened in 1984, a resoluteness filled the air. The young 49ers from the 1981 championship squad seemed to grasp that they had a finite number of years left to prove they were no one-season fluke, as skeptics claimed.

Eddie DeBartolo gave Bill Walsh leeway to load up and go for it. Walsh made trades to acquire expensive veteran depth. The draft yielded uber-talented rookies such as safety Jeff Fuller and nose tackle Michael Carter, who was late to camp because he was winning a shot-put silver medal at the Los Angeles Olympics.

Upshot? The 49ers became the first NFL team to win 15 games in a regular season, still a franchise record. Every Sunday when Joe Montana took his first center snap, it was like watching someone pull a trigger on an unstoppable weapon. Every Sunday when the 49ers defense lined up with skill and intent, opponents went nowhere.

Game after game, wonders abounded. In a playoff rematch against the Redskins, the 49ers racked up 534 total yards in a 37–31 victory. Twelve different 49ers scored touchdowns in the first six weeks of the season. Freddie Solomon scored TDs in 10 consecutive games. Montana missed two games with sore ribs, but backup Matt Cavanaugh filled in and won both. The 49ers defense was just as solid and vicious. The unit grew stronger still in November when pass rusher Fred Dean, a contract holdout, agreed to terms and demonstrated why he was the most feared pass rusher on the planet.

Walsh's X-and-O imagination received the most attention. One curious interviewer asked tight end Russ Francis to describe the West Coast Offense. "I could detail it in specifics but it's top secret," Francis joked. "We could have up to 120 pass plays installed for one game plan. It's sort of like reading the New York phone book."[60] The last part might honestly have been true. Walsh was in rare form. At times, he lined up offensive lineman Guy McIntyre as a blocking fullback.

The lone 1984 loss was to the bully Pittsburgh Steelers, who came to Candlestick and undid the 49ers' rhythm. Still, the score was tied at 17–17 late when Montana uncharacteristically threw into double coverage. A Pittsburgh linebacker intercepted, setting up the Steelers' winning field goal.

After finishing 15–1, the focused 49ers beat the New York Giants 21–10 in the playoffs, before powering through the vaunted Chicago Bears defense in the NFC Championship Game, winning 23–0. One obstacle remained.

Running back Wendell Tyler, left, runs behind the protection of Roger Craig during a 1984 game.

COURTESY OF GEORGE ROSE/GETTY IMAGES

Super Bowl XIX: Montana-Marino Matchup Mania

EVERYBODY SENSED where the NFL's 1984 postseason tournament was headed. The 15–1 Niners and the 14–2 Miami Dolphins were the two best teams with the two best records. And after the preliminaries were out of the way, they were the two Super Bowl XIX teams.

Which meant that the 49ers' Joe Montana and the Dolphins' Dan Marino were the two Super Bowl quarterbacks. Which meant that the camera-and-microphone mania leading up to the game would focus on them. Which meant that the two had to answer questions about the other in some fashion. Which they were loath to do.

Who could blame them? As Montana reminded people the week before the game: "I'm not playing against him. I'm playing against their defense. He's playing against our defense."[61]

Okay, whatever. Now, which of you two has the best throwing arm? Or the most beautiful girlfriend? Or the best tattoo? Either of you have a tattoo?

It was maddening for two guys who had much in common. Both grew up in the same quarterback-fertile soil of Western Pennsylvania that had spawned Hall of Famers Johnny Unitas and Joe Namath. Marino and Montana were both from Italian American families. Like Montana, Marino had been passed over in the NFL draft for other quarterbacks, finally selected after five others had come off the board.

Miami Dolphins quarterback Dan Marino wowed with his record-setting season in 1984.

COURTESY OF GEORGE GOJKOVICH/GETTY IMAGES

The difference was, entering the Super Bowl over-attention vortex, Marino was the hotter and sexier name. He was 23, in his second NFL season. Montana was old news. During the 1984 season, Marino had broken six NFL passing records, including for most TD passes (48) and most passing yards (5,084). In the Dolphins' two playoff games, he had thrown seven TD passes, five covering more than 30 yards.

The Sporting News

January 21, 1985

Price: $1.75

Brock, Wilhelm Step Into the Hall of Fame

Team-by-Team NBA, NHL Statistics

Shula and Walsh: A Pair of Super Coaches

SUPER BOWL JOE

Mr. Efficiency For the 49ers

COURTESY OF *THE SPORTING NEWS* VIA GETTY IMAGES

By comparison, Montana's otherwise-stellar numbers (28 touchdowns, 3,630 yards) were pedestrian. Bill Walsh saw that perception as disrespect.

"This week we are playing against the greatest passer of all time, as I understand it," Walsh said with sarcasm.[62]

"Everybody has their time," Montana said of Marino, "and this is his right now. I think this is great what's happening to him."[63]

"Everything Dan Marino does seems natural," said Miami coach Don Shula a few days before the Super Bowl XIX kickoff. "Nothing overwhelms him. He handles it."[64]

Shula should have added: So far.

Quarterback Joe Montana barks signals against the Miami Dolphins in Super Bowl XIX at Stanford Stadium.

COURTESY OF ICON SPORTSWIRE VIA GETTY IMAGES

Running back Roger Craig leaps over the line with the ball against the Miami Dolphins during Super Bowl XIX.
COURTESY OF FOCUS ON SPORT/GETTY IMAGES

January 20, 1985

Super Bowl XIX Proves a Point

SUPER BOWL XIX was not technically a home game for the 49ers. But close. Stanford Stadium was only 30 miles south of Candlestick Park and six miles from the team's Redwood City practice facility. The 49ers could sleep in their own beds the week of the game. The Miami Dolphins bunked out at a downtown Oakland hotel in a fishbowl environment.

This may or may not have contributed to the final score. But the "home game" mojo definitely added to the giddiness that consumed the region. Few fans could buy precious game tickets. The faithful went out and partied, anyway—all around the Bay.

Once the 84,059 ticket-holders settled onto their seat cushions with the Apple logo, provided by the nearby newish computer company to cover the stadium's splintered bleachers, anticipation was high for a wild offensive circus. Briefly, Montana and Marino gave it to them with matching touchdown drives. But then it was all 49ers.

The promised quarterback duel never materialized. Montana led three scoring drives in the second quarter while the defense completely stifled the mighty Miami offense. Bill Walsh and defensive coordinator George Seifert correctly diagnosed Miami's mediocre running game, so they alternated between five and six defensive backs on every down and dared Marino to solve the riddle.

Players lift coach Bill Walsh onto their shoulders after the 49ers' Super Bowl XIX victory.

COURTESY OF BETTMANN ARCHIVES VIA GETTY IMAGES

The 49ers outscored Miami 31–6 the rest of the way for a 38–16 statement victory. Marino completed 29 of 50 pass attempts for 318 yards with just the one touchdown and two interceptions while being sacked four times.

Montana was far more efficient, completing 24 of 35 attempts for 331 yards and three touchdowns. He also rushed for 59 yards and a touchdown and was named the game's MVP. Roger Craig scored three touchdowns—one rushing and two receiving—to set a Super Bowl record. The 49ers amassed 537 yards of offense, an average of 7.1 yards per play. They rightfully gloated afterward.

"The last two weeks, all we heard was how good Marino and his receivers were," Montana said. "Nobody said anything about our offense. It was all 'Stop Miami, stop Miami, stop Miami.' Nobody said that we would have to be stopped. Our offense was overlooked through the whole thing. I wanted to prove that we could match up against anyone."[65]

Hello, Jerry Rice

FOLLOWING THE second Super Bowl victory parade in four years, the 49ers weren't complacent. To win more Vince Lombardi trophies, they knew they needed an even better roster. And because San Francisco's status as the NFL's best team meant it wouldn't be high in the draft order, the front office could make zero mistakes.

Bill Walsh's attention was on wide receiver. Freddie Solomon's nagging injuries were causing him to miss playing time. A young replacement was needed.

That turned out to be Jerry Rice, who would become the greatest receiver in pro football history. Walsh had first heard about Rice on a 49ers' road trip to Houston while watching the sports report on a local television station. The report featured phenomenal highlights from a Mississippi Valley State game, all of them showing the school's receiving star, Rice. The 49ers coach was gobsmacked.

"He was sensational," Walsh said. "I vividly remember thinking, 'Damn, we're going to have to play against that guy.' I lay there wondering who was going to get him."[66]

Walsh decided it had to be the 49ers—in the first round. His scouts disagreed. They felt Rice had played against inferior competition and would still be available in the fifth round. Walsh wouldn't budge. He crafted a draft day trade to send the 49ers' first three picks to New England and moved up to select Rice at No. 16.

Rice was wide-eyed when he stepped off the plane from Mississippi. He had grown up in the rural hamlet of Crawford, where he'd worked for his bricklayer father. Jerry stood on scaffolding and caught the bricks tossed to him. At the start of the 1985 season, he had issues dropping footballs, which raised doubts before he was tutored by an unlikely person: Freddie Solomon, whom Rice had replaced in the starting lineup.

Jerry Rice is regarded as the greatest wide receiver ever to play the game.

COURTESY OF FOCUS ON SPORT/GETTY IMAGES

"He was our teammate," Solomon explained in 2010. "We all knew that Bill was going to play him. So, we needed him to get better for us to win—me included. I wasn't the only one who helped him. I think those dropped passes were just jitters. Jerry came in with the raw talent and all the tools. But he was still a rookie."[67]

Rice cemented his position forever in a breakout December game with 10 catches for 241 yards against the Los Angeles Rams. It was just a preview of coming attractions.

Roger Craig Bats 1,000 . . . and 1,000

ROGER CRAIG never really thought of himself as a pioneer. He thought of himself as a good running back, a reliable pass receiver, a fine pass blocker, and an all-around swell teammate.

That, of course, is what made him a pioneer. Because in 1985, he used all those tools to do something unprecedented: He was the first player in NFL history to gain more than 1,000 yards rushing and 1,000 yards receiving in the same season. In 1990, he became the first NFL running back to accumulate 500 career pass receptions.

It's crazy that Craig is not in the Pro Football Hall of Fame. Possibly, voters assumed that any running back could have stepped into Bill Walsh's dynamic offense and racked up silly stats. That's a preposterous notion. In the 40 years since Craig did so, only two players have matched his 1,000/1,000 feat: Marshall Faulk in 1999 and Christian McCaffrey in 2019.

It was no secret that Walsh loved swing passes and short flares to running backs. He was always on the lookout for someone who could take those modest passes and transform them into big gains.

At 6 foot and 222 pounds, Craig was big enough to hit the line hard, fast enough to run wide, and skilled enough to run sweet pass patterns, short and long. Once Jerry Rice joined the offense to go along with Joe Montana and Dwight Clark . . . well, good luck, opponents.

"Within our system, it was hard for defenses to cover all of us," Craig said. "It was like playing chess, and Montana was the guy who made all the checkmates."[68]

The 1985 season was an injury-besotted slog that saw the 49ers win 10 games before their playoff elimination by the New York Giants. Yet Craig was a steady force, gaining his 1,050 rushing yards on 214 carries and his 1,016 receiving yards on a then-record 92 catches. In the locker room after games when his jersey came off, Craig had welts and bruises covering his back and open sores on his arms. He often looked as if he had been run over by a fleet of motorcycles. But pioneers don't quit. They just keep pioneering, as Craig did.

Walsh called Roger Craig the best running back he'd ever coached. "He is a clear-cut Hall of Famer, and someday he will be honored as such," Walsh said.[69]

Roger Craig became the first player to accumulate 1,000 rushing yards and 1,000 receiving yards in the same season. The feat has been matched just twice since.

COURTESY OF DAVID MADISON/GETTY IMAGES

Joe Montana looks to pass against the Chicago Bears during the 1985 season.
COURTESY OF DAVID MADISON/GETTY IMAGES

Pain, Problems, Pressure

JOE MONTANA spent 1986 dining on a buffet of pain. After an arthroscopic shoulder operation in June, he recovered in time to start the first game at Tampa Bay. The 49ers won, but on one scramble rollout Montana contorted his spine as he threw across his body. It ruptured a disk in his lower back.

This meant more serious surgery. Ronnie Lott, seeing how difficult it was for Joe to move in the hospital, wondered if Montana's career was over. But four weeks later, Montana was upright and throwing footballs. Three weeks after that, doctors cleared him to play, though they advised caution. Montana was still suffering from foot and leg numbness. Bill Walsh wasn't sure what to do. "I had to really search my soul . . .," Walsh said. "I didn't want to be the one responsible for sending him out to get hurt even worse."[70]

Nose tackle Michael Carter (left) and defensive end Charles Haley were stalwarts of the 49ers defense.

COURTESY OF MICHAEL ZAGARIS/GETTY IMAGES

In Montana's absence, backup quarterback Jeff Kemp had performed well but injured his hip and was replaced by third-stringer Mike Moroski. The 49ers stood at 5–3–1 when Walsh bit his lip and put Montana in the lineup against St. Louis.

The mood at Candlestick Park that afternoon was a blend of fear and hope, like being at the circus and watching a high-wire act. Everybody held their breath. Montana didn't flinch. He threw three TD passes to Jerry Rice in a 43–17 rout. Seven weeks later, in the second quarter of a playoff game against the New York Giants, Montana was slammed to the ground. He spent the night in a hospital with a concussion while the Giants romped 49–3, the worst San Francisco playoff loss ever.

In 1987, the pain was more mental. After a crazy 27–26 victory over Cincinnati in Week 2—the 49ers had gotten the ball back with 2 seconds left, just enough time for a Montana-to-Rice touchdown—the NFL Players Association once more went on strike. The 49ers roster was divided. Fourteen players, including Montana, defied the union and reported to work. That created resentment. But when the work stoppage ended, the team coalesced and finished with a 13–2 record. Another Super Bowl was in the 49ers' sights.

They didn't make it past the first playoff game. Minnesota came to Candlestick and shocked the Niners, 36–24. Walsh benched a struggling Montana in the second half. He was replaced by the man who Walsh had acquired in case Montana was sidelined: Steve Young. It was the start of a classic NFL quarterback controversy.

Rice Can't Stop Catching Touchdowns

SANDWICHED BETWEEN their Super Bowl wins, the 49ers endured three seasons in the mid-'80s that began with hope and ended just short of Vince Lombardi hardware. Throughout it all, there was one consistent theme: When in doubt, send the ball toward Jerry Rice. He'll make cool stuff happen.

This was especially the case in 1987, when Rice set an NFL record with 22 TD receptions. That mark has since been surpassed just once, by Randy Moss with 23 touchdowns in 2007. But because of the 1987 players' strike, Rice accomplished his feat in only 12 games on 65 receptions. He also scored a rushing touchdown on an end-around.

Anyone watching Rice that season saw him at the height of his powers, averaging 16.6 yards per catch and making defensive backs curse. Rice was always reaching. For receptions. For the goal line. For all-around excellence, blocking downfield or running his patterns or leaping for the ball. In that era, there was no more elegant sight in sports. He aspired to be the best player to ever play his position and succeeded. It began with the way he drove himself in practice.

"I think it would blow people away to know how hard Jerry works during the week," said 49ers tight end Brent Jones. "I've heard how other guys at his level, on other teams, take days off whenever they want, even if they're not hurt that bad. Jerry runs hard. Every play. Every day."[71]

Rice owned nearly every wide receiving record by the end of his career. But his 1987 single-season touchdown record showcased his most underrated quality: an ability to not be tackled inside the 5-yard line. If the ball was in his hands, Rice would always make it to the end zone. Four times that season, he scored three touchdowns in a game.

Jerry Rice seemed to be superhuman in 1987 as he caught 22 TD passes. He poses for a portrait in 1990.
COURTESY OF JIM GENSHEIMER/ *MERCURY NEWS WEST MAGAZINE*

As a younger player, he was soft-spoken, but became more blunt as he matured.

"I have people tell me that when they see me on television, I always seem happy," Rice said. "And I am, mostly. But deep down inside, I can be a monster. . . Once you score a touchdown, that defensive back knows you have him under control. I never spin the ball on the ground after I score. I did my job, and it's over. That's it. That's all."[72]

1987

Hi Joe, I'm Steve

WHEN STEVE Young was traded from Tampa Bay to San Francisco on April 24, 1987, alarm bells did not immediately go off. Then, as the drama of a quarterback controversy unfolded, opinions exploded. People took sides, for Montana or for Young. Through it all, the team kept winning.

Young had already been through a football wringer before joining the 49ers. After setting records at Brigham Young University, he spurned the NFL draft to sign with the upstart USFL's Los Angeles Express franchise. When the USFL folded two years later, the Buccaneers claimed Young in a special supplemental draft. In both L.A. and Tampa, he played behind shaky offensive lines in shoddy offenses. Young spent every week scrambling relentlessly to avoid hospitalization. This gave him a label of being "one dimensional." On the positive side, he was staying alive.

Enter the 49ers in the spring of 1987. After watching Joe Montana's 1986 medical obstacle course, Bill Walsh was convinced that Joe would not be his quarterback for much longer. Walsh wanted a Plan B. The team sent second- and fourth-round picks to Tampa—plus a million DeBartolo dollars—in exchange for Young. Walsh told Young he'd soon be the 49ers starter because Montana was likely on his last legs. When Young flew to the Bay Area for his first 49er workout, he noticed that Joe's back and legs looked pretty good. Young even had to borrow Montana's size 11 shoes for the workout, almost too perfect a metaphor.

After Young replaced Montana and produced two touchdowns in the shocking 1987 playoff loss to Minnesota, the 1988 preseason began with a froth of quarterback uncertainty. Walsh didn't squash it, saying he planned to use both men as the autumn unfurled.

Joe Montana and Steve Young go over plays with quarterbacks coach Mike Holmgren.

COURTESY OF MICHAEL ZAGARIS

"It isn't something we'll do out of desperation," Walsh told a reporter. "You can do some things with Steve you can't do with anybody else. But when and how?"[73]

Montana started the 1988 opener at New Orleans but injured an elbow in the victory, so Young started in Week 2 against the Giants. At halftime, with the score tied, Walsh switched up and inserted Montana. Joe's last-minute TD pass to Jerry Rice won the game. In the locker room, both quarterbacks were asked if they were prepared to handle such back-and-forth the rest of the way.

"I don't have any choice," Montana said with a semi-rueful smile.

"Sure," said Young, standing two lockers away. "If that's what he asks us to do."[74]

You could hear faint alarm bells.

October 30, 1988

Steve Young's Long and Winding Touchdown Run

THROUGHOUT THE 1988 season, Joe Montana and Steve Young kept alternating at quarterback while the team kept alternating wins and losses. No one was sure where things were headed. But there was plenty of entertainment along the way

In Week 9 against the Minnesota Vikings, Young turned an NFL playing surface into a drunk pinball machine, featuring him as the silver ball. Montana's back was acting up, so Young played the entire game. But he and the Niners trailed 21–17 with less than two minutes remaining.

On third down at the Viking 49-yard line, Young dropped back to pass. His primary receiver was supposed to be Mike Wilson on a curl pattern. But Wilson was covered. Young began scanning for other options. He saw only Minnesota pass rushers.

Twenty-one seconds of insanity commenced. Young did a full 360-degree spin, spied open grass and took off. He weaved right, escaped one tackle, cut back left, and escaped two more. And kept weaving. On the radio, broadcaster Lon Simmons was apoplectic as he described the action, screaming: "He's going to be sacked! No! Gets away! He runs! Gets away again!"

Finally, as Jerry Rice threw a block to wipe out the last potential Vikings tackler, Young broke free inside the 15-yard line. But his legs started to buckle. Young staggered the last five yards before a lunging dive across the goal line for the deciding touchdown in a 24–21 victory.

"He looked like he was about to die of a heart attack going into the end zone," said lineman Randy Cross.[75]

COURTESY OF MATTHEW J. LEE/*OAKLAND TRIBUNE*/MEDIANEWS GROUP VIA GETTY IMAGES

Steve Young scrambles, then stumbles into the end zone in a wild 49-yard run against the Minnesota Vikings.

COURTESY OF TOM LEVY/*SAN FRANCISCO CHRONICLE* VIA GETTY IMAGES

"I couldn't get my legs out in front of me," Young said. "My legs died. I'm glad I was only on the 5."[76]

A laughing Montana greeted Young on the sideline and said, "I know I couldn't have made it. I would have passed out long before that."[77] Young then credited Montana for helping him with advice during the game. At a thorny time when the two men were working through a thicket of competitive ambition and ego, it was a sweet interlude.

A fast-food television commercial in 2006 superimposed the Burger King mascot over Young's body on the 49-yard highlight play. It still wasn't as nutty as the real thing.

Beating the Unbeatable Bears

BY ALL rights, the 49ers' third Super Bowl trip should not have happened. In mid-November, their record was 6–5. The optics were worse. The fifth defeat was a 9–3 loss to the Raiders. The Niners had gone five quarters without a touchdown. Eddie DeBartolo was upbraiding his head coach on a regular basis, threatening to fire Walsh any time in the next five minutes.

The five minutes turned into never. The 49ers ripped off a four-game winning streak to clinch the NFC West. Then they beat Minnesota 34–6 in their first playoff game. But the next step seemed to be insurmountable.

The NFC title game was set for Chicago's Soldier Field against the Bears in the heyday of coach Mike Ditka's kick-butt tenure. The 49ers had never won a January playoff game away from home. A game day temperature of 20 degrees—wind chill two degrees above zero—made the task more frigidly ridiculous.

Except, sorry, wrong again. Joe Montana, now locked in as the starting quarterback, managed the Bears' blitzing defense with aplomb and hooked up with Jerry Rice twice for touchdowns in the first half. Two more 49er touchdowns in the second half clinched it, as the Bears managed just one field goal all day.

Final score: Niners 28, Bears 3. Super Bowl next stop.

"I can name five or six things that were impossible about this game for us, that we weren't supposed to be able to do," Bill Walsh said afterward. "But we did it."[78]

"I think this is one of the best games for all of us in a while," Montana said. Asked if there had been a time when he wondered if he'd ever get back to a Super Bowl, Montana grinned and said: "Yeah, every year."[79]

Another matchup against the Cincinnati Bengals lay ahead. Rumors circulated that Walsh would retire if his team won. As Walsh headed for the team bus, a reporter observed that he seemed giddier than at any time in his career.

"Maybe I can see the end," Walsh said, his eyes brightening. "It's like *The Wizard of Oz*, and you can see the end of the yellow brick road."[80]

Running back Roger Craig (left), fullback Tom Rathman, and receiver Jerry Rice celebrate Rathman's touchdown against the Bears at Soldier Field to win the NFC title.

COURTESY OF BETTMANN ARCHIVES VIA GETTY IMAGES

Jerry Rice breaks free from a Bengals defender during Super Bowl XXIII. Rice was named the game's MVP.

COURTESY OF RICH PILLING/*THE SPORTING NEWS* VIA GETTY IMAGES

Super Bowl XXIII: Facing Familiar Foes

SUPER BOWL XXIII was a rematch of Super Bowl XVI in an entirely different setting. This time the 49ers would face the Cincinnati Bengals in tropical weather, at Miami's Joe Robbie Stadium. Once again Walsh would face his old team, who now were coached by creative Sam Wyche, who had played for Walsh in Cincinnati and then tutored Montana as a 49er assistant.

Super Bowl Week, always a spectacle, was dominated that year by ominous fire and speculation. The fire came from riots in Miami's Overtown neighborhood, set off when a Black motorcyclist was shot by a police officer. The 49ers were staying far away at a Miami airport hotel, but the Bengals' team hotel was just 10 blocks from the trouble. It created an uneasy mood, full of speculation in the days leading up to the game.

Walsh had hinted that he might be resigning after the game, though his remarks on the topic were cagey. Other rumors spread that Jerry Rice's sore ankle might keep him out of the lineup, even after Rice was spotted dancing at a local club.

"I'm down here to have fun," Rice said. "I danced but didn't do anything fancy. Everything was straight ahead."[81]

Lastly, there was talk that Montana, with his physical issues and the controversy involving Young, was not the quarterback he had been in his first two Super Bowl games. Joe was definitely on the spot to re-convince and re-silence his doubters.

All would be revealed at kickoff time in what was expected to be a high-scoring game. The 49ers had racked up nine touchdowns in their two playoff games. The Bengals had the league MVP in quarterback Boomer Esiason as well as flashy rookie running back Ickey Woods.

The scoring orgy failed to materialize. The halftime score was 3–3. Both teams struggled to find a rhythm. The third quarter wasn't much better, with matching field goals and a 93-yard kickoff return for a touchdown by Cincinnati's Stanford Jennings. Ronnie Lott made a statement with a thundering tackle of Ickey Woods, rendering him ineffective the rest of the game. With the score tied at 13–13 in the fourth quarter, the Bengals' Jim Breech kicked another field goal to give his team the 16–13 lead.

JIM BORGMAN/*THE CINCINNATI ENQUIRER*

COURTESY OF ROB BROWN/ GETTY IMAGES

Wide receiver John Taylor catches a touchdown pass with just seconds left to go to clinch the 49ers' 20–16 victory over the Bengals in Super Bowl XXIII.

COURTESY OF ROBERT RIGER/GETTY IMAGES

January 22, 1989

Super Bowl XXIII: The Drive and Candy Comeback

TRUE STORY. When the ball sailed over the crossbar to give the Cincinnati Bengals a three-point lead with 3 minutes, 20 seconds left to play in Super Bowl XXIII, Steve Young turned to Joe Montana and said, "Well, it's set up perfectly for us."[82]

Which it was. Montana was going to take the field and move the 49ers into the west end zone at Joe Robbie Stadium, no matter what.

A penalty forced the 49ers to start their drive at their own 8-yard line. There was a long television timeout. That's when Montana tried to relax a nervous Harris Barton in the huddle by nudging him and saying: "Hey, H, check it out. Look over there in that end zone . . . hey, there's John Candy."[83]

When play resumed, though, Joe was coolly locked in, as usual. He moved the 49ers in small chunks, a pass here, a run there. Montana was in disbelief that the Bengals' secondary was mostly playing man-to-man defense against Jerry Rice. That was an open invitation.

Montana had just one incompletion in the drive. He hyperventilated and needed to clear his head, so he purposely threw the ball out of bounds. Then, passes to Rice and Roger Craig landed the 49ers at the 10-yard line.

The next play call was 20 Halfback Curl X Up. But at the scrimmage line, the 49er running backs lined up incorrectly, taking primary target Craig out of the picture. Rice, in motion, was also covered. Montana saw John Taylor slanting across the end zone in front of a safety and behind a cornerback. Touchdown. Taylor's only reception of the day came with 34 seconds left on the clock. The 49ers won 20–16, seizing their third Super Bowl title in eight years.

"Joe Montana is not human," said Cincinnati receiver Cris Collinsworth. "I don't want to call him a god, but he's definitely somewhere in between."[84]

Joe Montana led a drive for the ages to win Super Bowl XXIII.
COURTESY OF FOCUS ON SPORT/GETTY IMAGES

Bengals coach Sam Wyche, left, and 49ers coach Bill Walsh embrace after the game.
COURTESY OF MICHAEL E. KEATING/*THE CINCINNATI ENQUIRER*

Rice, with 11 catches for 215 yards and a touchdown, was named the game's MVP. Walsh and Wyche hugged after the game. At the postgame trophy ceremony, broadcaster Brent Musburger asked Walsh if he had coached his last 49ers game. Walsh couldn't answer. He emotionally collapsed into the arms of his son, who was standing alongside.

Montana, asked to describe his feelings, answered: "As big as words can go."[85]

Walsh Passes the Baton to Seifert

THE SETTING was a hotel ballroom in Monterey, California, 100 miles from Candlestick Park. It was an unexpected location for a baton pass by a Super Bowl champ. But that's where Bill Walsh completed the handoff to George Seifert, who would coach the 49ers for the next eight seasons.

Two days after the Super Bowl victory parade in San Francisco, Walsh drove down the coast for a meeting with Eddie DeBartolo, who was playing in a golf tournament. Walsh said he was retiring as head coach. DeBartolo tried to talk Walsh out of quitting by offering him a raise. But Walsh stood firm. Ten years as a head coach had sapped him. Walsh's personal life also played a role in his decision. His wife, Geri, was pressing him to step away.

"I had a choice to quit coaching or to quit being married," Walsh told author David Harris.[86]

The next move was logical. Walsh agreed to stay on as a 49ers vice president of football operations. He convinced DeBartolo to replace him with Seifert, Walsh's trusted defensive coordinator for a unit that had just allowed one offensive touchdown over three postseason games. Seifert was on his way to Cleveland to interview for the Browns' coaching vacancy when he heard about DeBartolo's offer and immediately took a plane back to the Bay. The deal was wrapped up quickly. The news conference was set up the next day, televised live from the Monterey ballroom.

Seifert was droll when asked how he felt about the whole thing. "As my wife told me just before the playoffs, 'Don't screw it up, George,'" he said.[87]

The mood was lighthearted. Walsh's face showed no trace of the jagged nerve endings and strain that had been evident over the previous few months.

Seifert was naturally happy to inherit a bountiful roster, the result of his predecessor's eye for talent. Three years earlier, Walsh had made six draft-day trades to stack up 14 picks, then used them to select consequential players such as fullback Tom Rathman, cornerback Tim McKyer, wide receiver John Taylor, and pass rusher Charles Haley. All had contributed to the Super Bowl run.

"I'm still in kind of a euphoric situation," Seifert said. "I haven't lost a game yet, and nobody has lost a big office bet because of something I did."[88]

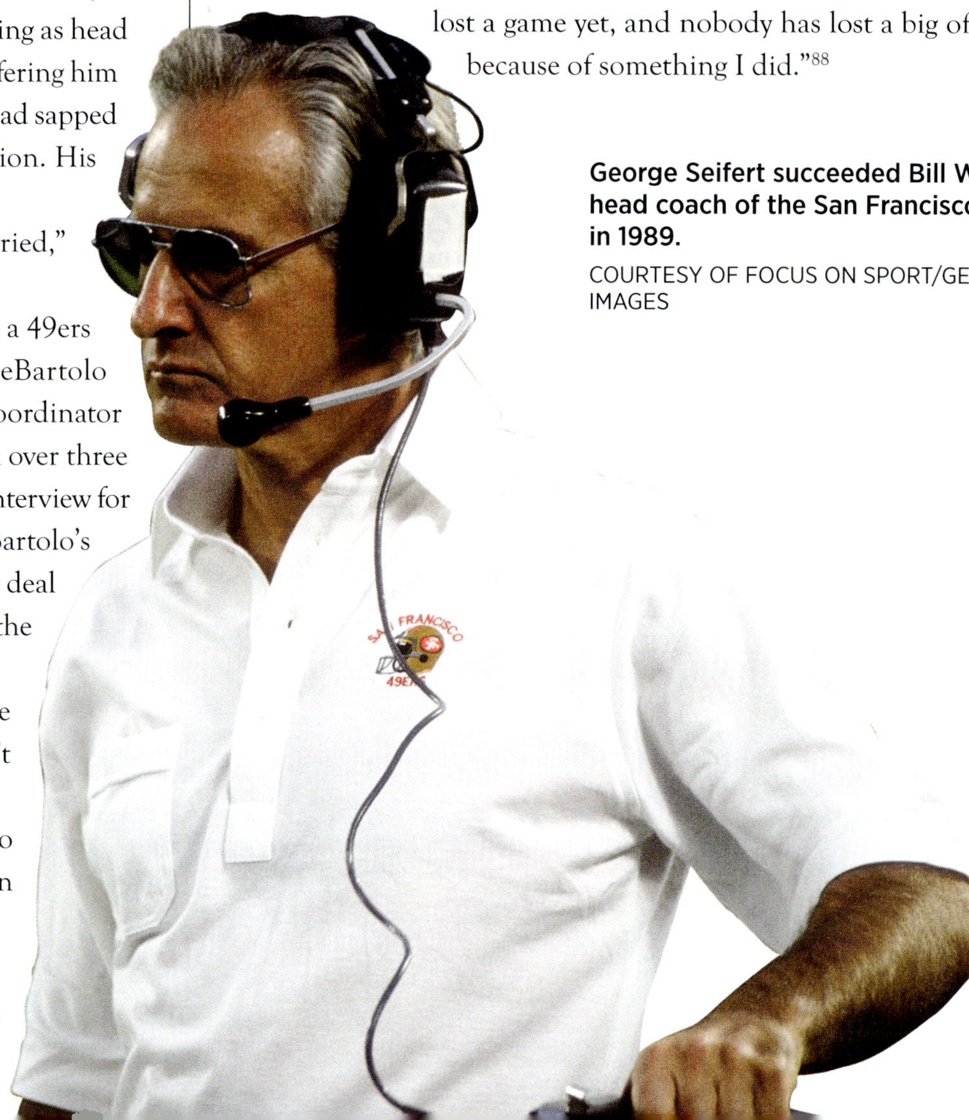

George Seifert succeeded Bill Walsh as head coach of the San Francisco 49ers in 1989.

COURTESY OF FOCUS ON SPORT/GETTY IMAGES

September 24, 1989

Joe's Philadelphia Story

IF PRESSED, many 1989 Niners would admit it off the record. One of their big motivations that season was showing the world they could win a championship without Bill Walsh.

A September game in Philadelphia convinced them it was very possible. Some people call it Joe Montana's finest hour. The Niners had won their first two games of the season, but they knew the Eagles were a Super Bowl contender. Philadelphia was coached by the brash Buddy Ryan, who wasn't impressed by Montana's reputation.

"It's hard to throw the football running on your butt, you know," Ryan said on a Philly radio talk show before the game. "They're the world champs, but we're not afraid of them."[89]

His team backed up Ryan's words. Philadelphia's All-Pro defensive lineman, Reggie White, roamed freely and ferociously. In the first three quarters, Montana was sacked seven times, tripped himself twice while dropping back, and stumbled backward into his own end zone for a safety. The Niners trailed 21–10 early in the fourth quarter when Montana released a TD pass to John Taylor but took another crushing hit in the process. Joe went down hard and wasn't moving.

"Worried? Oh, hell, yes, we were worried," said offensive tackle Harris Barton. "Joe gets that glazed look in his eyes, and you know he's been shellacked. Then three guys help him up . . . We'd get to the sidelines and Joe would say, 'Okay, let's get this thing settled down.' I was just amazed that he could line up at all after getting smacked in the head by Reggie White."[90]

After a quick checkup by team doctors, Montana stayed in the game. He threw three more TD passes, to Tom Rathman, Brent Jones, and Jerry Rice. In the fourth quarter alone, Montana completed 11 of 12 attempts for 227 yards and four touchdowns. He also ran for 19 yards. The 49ers walked off the field a 38–28 winner.

Top: Philadelphia Eagles defensive end Reggie White sacks Joe Montana during a tough matchup in 1989.

Bottom: John Taylor outruns the Eagles at Veterans Stadium.

COURTESY OF FOCUS ON SPORT/GETTY IMAGES

At his locker after the game, Montana did his version of trash talking. "They won the first half," he said. "I won the second half."[91]

By season's end, Montana would post the highest quarterback rating (112.4) and third-highest completion percentage (70.2%) in NFL history. Bill Walsh called none of the plays.

October 22, 1989

The Quake and the Ugly Crack

ON OCTOBER 17, 1989, the San Francisco Giants and Oakland A's were preparing for Game 3 of the World Series when a 6.9 tremblor struck the Bay Area. Dwight Clark was with Joe Montana and his family at Candlestick Park when the rumble hit before the first pitch. They evacuated safely, but structural damage to the stadium forced the Series to be delayed and relocated the 49ers' next home game, five days later, to Stanford Stadium.

More than 70,000 people—larger than Candlestick's capacity—bought tickets to see the contest between the 49ers and the New England Patriots. The fans were seeking a respite from the anxiety and stress of the earthquake, which had resulted in 63 deaths and thousands of injuries. Instead, they were reminded how violent and dangerous football can be.

On the game's second play, 49ers safety Jeff Fuller collided head-on with New England running back John Stephens. A loud "crack" of helmet-to-helmet contact carried to the stadium's top row. Stephens groggily pulled himself to his feet. Fuller didn't. He wasn't moving.

As trainers and doctors rushed onto the field, one of them reached into Fuller's mouth and pried his tongue out of his throat. Standing nearby, Ronnie Lott turned to Eric Wright and said, "I don't think Jeff is going to be all right."[92]

An ambulance from Stanford Hospital pulled onto the turf as coach George Seifert and medical personnel did what they could. Linebacker Keena Turner organized a huddled prayer. A small oxygen tank pumped air into Fuller. Seifert looked as if he wanted to jump into the ambulance with him for the ride to the hospital but was waved off. Action resumed. But not without another injury. In the second quarter, Montana absorbed a helmet-to-knee hit and had to ride a cart off the field.

An earthquake cancelled Game 3 of the World Series at Candlestick Park on October 17, 1989.
COURTESY OF BETTMANN ARCHIVES VIA GETTY IMAGES

Steve Young took over under center. He finished the game in terrific fashion, completing 11 of 12 passes with three touchdowns in a 37–20 victory. The crowd's biggest cheer, though, erupted when Montana emerged from the locker room in the fourth quarter and stood by the 49ers' bench. Young wasn't upset.

"They *should* applaud," Young said. "I would, too. He'd gone out on a stretcher. It was remarkable to see him back on the sidelines."[93]

Fuller wasn't as fortunate. He regained feeling in his legs but suffered two broken neck vertebrae and severed nerves, causing his right arm to be partially paralyzed. It didn't recover. He never played another game.

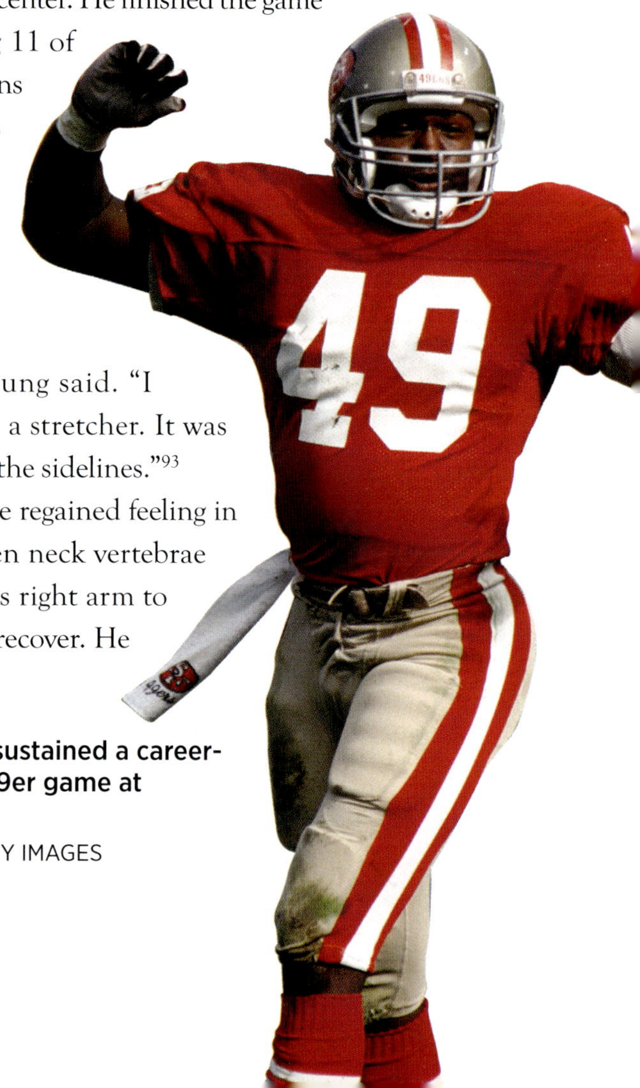

Hard-hitting safety Jeff Fuller sustained a career-ending spinal injury during a 49er game at Stanford Stadium in 1989.
COURTESY OF GEORGE ROSE/GETTY IMAGES

December 11, 1989

John Taylor's Monday Night Special

OF THE 49ers' championship wide receivers in the late 1980s, Jerry Rice was always going to be Batman with John Taylor cast as Robin. But for one December night in 1989, Robin produced his own prime time special.

In Week 14, the Los Angeles Rams were strong challengers for the NFC West lead. A *Monday Night Football* game in Anaheim would end up deciding the division winner. And Taylor would be the most decisive decider. Under the bright lights, Taylor caught 11 passes that covered 286 yards, including two touchdowns of more than 90 yards each.

"It was unbelievable," Taylor said. "It's something that I never thought would happen, something you always dream about."[94]

For the Rams, a nightmare. They had a 17-point lead in the fourth quarter when the 49ers stormed back with three touchdowns to win 30–27. Taylor's dramatic TD was the game's turning point.

With 6:27 remaining, the Rams were ahead 27–17 and threatening to score. Then quarterback Jim Everett fumbled the snap, and the 49ers recovered on their own 5-yard line. On first down, Taylor ran a shallow slant pattern. Joe Montana hit him eight yards downfield. Taylor took care of the next 87 yards. He ran through three tackles and sprinted up the right sideline. Batman threw the last block to spring Robin into the end zone.

In just two plays, the Rams had gone from potentially clinching victory to clutching their throats. They were defeated long before Roger Craig scored the actual winning touchdown a few minutes later. Earlier in the game, Taylor had scored a 92-yard touchdown that followed the same theme. He grabbed a short pass and used his legs to cover the rest of the way.

John Taylor ran through the Los Angeles Rams defense for two touchdowns of 90-plus yards during *Monday Night Football*.

COURTESY OF MICHAEL ZAGARIS/GETTY IMAGES

The game was a high-water mark for a player who had been drafted primarily as a kick returner from obscure Delaware State. Taylor had grown up outside Philadelphia in Pennsauken, New Jersey, where he had played touch football in a neighborhood cemetery because it was the only real open space. In college, 33 of his 100 receptions were TD catches. You might call that foreshadowing.

Taylor's nine-year 49ers deployment created numerous oh-wow moments, including two punt return touchdowns and his winning Super Bowl XXIII grab. But his Monday Night Special stood apart.

Roger Craig's signature high-stepping knees made him difficult to tackle during his tenure with the San Francisco 49ers.

COURTESY OF OTTO GREULE JR./ALLSPORT/ GETTY IMAGES

Candlestick Coolness

CANDLESTICK PARK, by unanimous agreement, was a dump. Yet paradoxically, for a solid chunk of the 1980s, Candlestick was also the grooviest place in the NFL.

Some of it was the fashionable tailgating, full of Northern California wine tastings and fresh crab dip. Some of it was the view of San Francisco Bay. Some of it was the way wispy fog would drift over and through the stadium light towers during a night game, bringing a spooky vibe to the proceedings below.

The coolest of the coolness, though, occurred on the field and in the seats. The Candlestick concourses may have been crowded and damp, with too few restrooms and too many overserved patrons. But the 49ers' success in the decade brought celebrities out of the woodwork, whether they were true football fans or simply in town to shoot a blockbuster.

You never knew who might visit the pregame sidelines on any given Sunday. Julia Roberts? Robin Williams? The cast of *Full House*? All claimed 49er fandom. Teri Hatcher had an up-close view of the action as a member of the Gold Rush cheerleading squad before ascending to television and film stardom.

Huey Lewis and the News frequently sang the national anthem at Candlestick.

COURTESY OF MICHAEL OLMSTEAD AND E2K PRODUCTIONS

Meanwhile, the halftime shows rocked. Long before the league embraced the idea, team entertainment coordinator Michael Olmstead booked Bay Area acts such as Greg Kihn, Starship, and The Tubes to play between the second and third quarters.

One band, Huey Lewis and the News, had the most lasting connection with the team thanks to a close friendship with Dwight Clark and Joe Montana. Lewis and his band traditionally performed the national anthem before big games and were even invited along on a few team charter flights. In return, Lewis invited Clark, Montana, Ronnie Lott, and others to sing backup on their hit song, "Hip to Be Square."

Wisely, the players didn't quit their day jobs.

Actress Teri Hatcher was a member of the Gold Rush cheerleaders.

COURTESY OF MICHAEL OLMSTEAD AND E2K PRODUCTIONS

Charles Haley pursues Philadelphia Eagles quarterback Randall Cunningham in a 1989 game.
COURTESY OF FOCUS ON SPORT/GETTY IMAGES

Team of the Eighties

NO JUDGE or jury decides which NFL franchise gets to call itself a Team of the Decade. It generally happens by popular acclaim. The 49ers owned the 1980s, by acclamation and facts. By 1989, they had already won three Super Bowls in the decade and were headed for their fourth.

As the team rolled to another division title with a 14–2 record, the more relevant debate was whether it could surpass the 1984 Niners. The 1984 team had the best regular season record (15–1). But Joe Montana's best statistical quarterbacking season was 1989, en route to winning the league MVP. The 1989 team's only two losses were by one point to the Rams and by four points to the Packers. They won their three postseason games by an average of 33 points.

Plus, there were all those fourth-quarter comeback victories, in Tampa and Philadelphia and Anaheim. "We've got the best team in football in the last two minutes of a game," Roger Craig said.[95]

The other 58 minutes weren't bad, either. After leaving coaching, Bill Walsh had accepted an offer to be NBC's lead NFL analyst. During a 1989 mid-season San Francisco game telecast, he was asked which of the three Super Bowl championship teams that he'd coached had been the best. Walsh chose none of the above. "Oh, I think this year's 49er team is the best one," he said.[96]

All the Niners needed to do was prove it by winning another title. But everybody could see that coming. Walsh may have been gone, but the staff structure he'd assembled—including general manager John McVay and longtime assistant coaches Bobb McKittrick and Bill McPherson—remained big parts of the machinery that supported George Seifert.

The 49ers are unlikely to ever match their supremacy of the Eighties. When the decade began, the team possessed zero Vince Lombardi trophies. By the end of the decade, they owned four Lombardis, the most productive wide receiver of all time, and the most thrilling clutch time QB in the game. The 49ers, in the phraseology of a popular new 1989 situation comedy, were masters of their domain.

Gold Rush cheerleaders show off the Lombardi Trophy.

COURTESY OF GEORGE ROSE/GETTY IMAGES

Joe Montana and the 49ers dismantle the No. 1-ranked Denver Broncos defense in Super Bowl XXIV at the Superdome in New Orleans.
COURTESY OF GIN ELLIS/ GETTY IMAGES

Super Bowl XXIV: Not Even Close

THE OBLITERATION was total and complete. And it was only halftime. The 49ers led on the scoreboard, 27–3. Joe Montana and Jerry Rice were basically playing pitch and catch. The Denver Broncos were allegedly playing defense. As if it mattered. In Super Bowl XXIV, Montana and Rice and the entire 49ers offense existed in their own space-time continuum, from the opening drive onward.

That first drive concluded when Montana dropped back from the 20-yard line and noticed Rice coming free on a delay pattern over the middle. Pass. Catch.

But then came the best part. The week before the game, the Broncos had talked about how big and strong their defensive backs were compared to most teams, how hard they hit. So here was Rice, snaring the ball in open space at the 7-yard line. And here came Denver safety Steve Atwater, taller and heavier than Rice. Atwater slammed into Rice full force, full frontal. Atwater went down. Rice remained upright. He spun away into the end zone. Six points.

"I was pumped up," said Rice, who had noticed on film that Denver's safeties didn't wrap up and tackle ball carriers, just ran into them and thought that would be enough. "When I get the ball, I'm not just going down. You have to knock me down."[97]

Eddie DeBartolo was sitting with the retired Bill Walsh in a Superdome luxury suite. Five minutes into the game, Walsh turned to DeBartolo and said, "You can go home . . . Eddie, they can't cover anybody . . . This game is going to be a blowout."[98]

DeBartolo decided to stay. He saw all five touchdowns thrown by Montana, a Super Bowl record. He saw Rice's three TD catches, also a Super Bowl record. He saw the six other Super Bowl records that the 49ers either set or tied that afternoon in a 55–10 beatdown that to this day is the largest margin of victory in any Super Bowl game. The eight 49er touchdowns are also a record. Montana won his third Super Bowl MVP award with 22 completions in 29 attempts for 297 yards.

The Denver Broncos were outmatched by the 49ers on offense and defense in Super Bowl XXIV.
COURTESY OF RICK STEWART/ALLSPORT/GETTY IMAGES

"Every time we came off the field, we were saying, 'They can't stop us, they can't stop us,'" remembered fullback Tom Rathman, who ran for two touchdowns.[99]

Super Bowl XXIV spoiled fans of the 49ers for the rest of their lives. Ever since, they have expected the team to match that 55–10 standard of awesomeness every week. Only dynasties have that problem.

Jerry Rice and his teammates celebrate another score. The 49ers beat the Broncos 55–10 in Super Bowl XXIV.
COURTESY OF FOCUS ON SPORT/GETTY IMAGES

Joe Montana was hit hard in the 1990 NFC Championship Game against the New York Giants.

COURTESY OF DAN HONDA VIA GETTY IMAGES

1990

The "What If" Season

FOR ANY other NFL franchise, 1990 would have been considered a magnificent season. The 49ers won their first 10 games on the way to a 14–2 record. In October, Jerry Rice caught five TD passes in a 45–35 victory at Atlanta, tying an NFL record. The Niners' 13th straight road win set another league record. As did their 18th straight overall win, in Week 11 at home against Tampa Bay.

Throughout that autumn at Candlestick Park, the Niners were swarmed with adoration. On the road, it was like traveling with the Beatles or Rolling Stones, as fans camped in front of the team hotels to catch a glimpse of the star players.

And week after week, month after month, thrumming background music kept repeating the same lyric: "Threepeat, threepeat, threepeat." No NFL team had ever won three consecutive Super Bowls. The 49ers didn't run away from the challenge. "It's a part of everybody's mind because we have that opportunity," said Joe Montana. "But we can't look to the end of the season . . . We have a lot of tough games."[100]

The toughest were later. The 49ers finally lost one, in November against the Rams. In December, they faced the New York Giants in one of the most physical, body-banging contests ever seen at Candlestick and managed to grind out a 7–3 win. When the Niners laid a 28–10 number on Washington in their first playoff game, it set up a rematch with the Giants for the NFC Championship.

In another smash fest, only one touchdown was scored in the entire game, on a 61-yard pass from Montana to John Taylor. Then a blindside hit of Montana bruised his sternum and broke his hand. Young took over. The Niners led 13–12 with three minutes remaining when Roger Craig fumbled away the ball. The Giants won on a 42-yard field goal as time expired. The threepeat was dead. "We were as close as you can get," Young said.[101]

Craig never let the fumble define his career. "It was just one play," he said. "That's part of the game. It wasn't meant to be. Joe got hurt. The defense couldn't stop them. There's never one play where you win or lose."[102]

Here's what nobody realized as they left Candlestick that day: Montana would never start another game for the 49ers. And both Craig and Ronnie Lott had played their last games for the team.

San Francisco 49ers quarterback Steve Young uses his legs against the Minnesota Vikings in a 1997 game.
COURTESY OF JOHN G. MABANGLO/AFP VIA GETTY IMAGES

CHAPTER 4

FINDING NEW FOOTING

1991–1998

AFTER THEIR FOUR Super Bowl victories in the 1980s, the 49ers had a high bar to clear to produce another championship decade. They were modestly successful.

On the field, the cast changed dramatically. By 1990, only five players were left from the 1981 Super Bowl champs: Ronnie Lott, Joe Montana, Keena Turner, Mike Wilson, and Eric Wright. By 1991, all but Montana were gone. He and Steve Young then endured a quarterbacking soap opera that never seemed to end, until it did, with Joe's stunning departure. New faces Ricky Watters, Bryant Young, and Ken Norton Jr. surfaced and excelled. Deion Sanders even made a cameo appearance.

Off the field, the front office made a strange decision in 1991 to replace the classic "SF" helmet design with a bold "49ers" decal. The move went over about as well as New Coke or the AMC Pacer. After public outcry, the "new" 49ers logo died a quick death. Oh, yes. In 1994, at a Candlestick Park concession stand, garlic fries were introduced to the world. The new delicacy may or may not have contributed to the team's fifth Super Bowl ring. >>>

Farewell to Dynasty Makers, but Not to QB Drama

THINGS GOT very weird for the 49ers in 1991. First, the helmet logo fiasco. Then, two stout fenceposts of their dynasty team walked out the door. And the 49ers didn't stop them. Under new NFL "Plan B" rules, teams had to submit a list of 20 players under contract who could become unrestricted free agents. The Niners' list included Ronnie Lott and Roger Craig. Too old? Too banged up? The Raiders didn't think so. They gave both men rich deals.

But that still wasn't the weirdest thing that happened in 1991. The Niners ended up almost making the playoffs with Steve Bono at quarterback, though most fans were more busy picking sides in the Joe Montana–Steve Young quarterback debate that began in the preseason.

The short-lived new 49ers logo in 1991
COURTESY OF MARK PURDY

Head coach George Seifert was strongly in favor of both sides. In the offseason, he said that Montana was the team's starter. On the other hand, Seifert also said he was happy that Steve Young had signed a new two-year contract with the 49ers. When the deal was announced, Young said, "The bottom line is, they expect me to play and I expect to play. I didn't sign to sit down."[103]

Montana, obviously, was not consulted. He admitted to "animosity" between them. "Steve is on a big push for himself," Montana said. "I can say we only have a working relationship. That's all it is."[104]

In the Bay, Team Joe had more fan support than Team Steve. Except, wait, what? Another plot twist! At summer training camp, Montana felt pain in his throwing elbow. He was put on injured reserve and underwent surgery for a torn pronator tendon. Young was QB1. He racked up good statistics while steering the 49ers to a rocky 4–4 start.

But in Week 10 at Atlanta, Young was hauled down and sprained his left knee. Bono jumped in and surprisingly led the Niners to five straight wins—before spraining his own knee. Young returned for the finale against Chicago, a 52–14 rout, and led the league with a 101.8 passer rating. However, the team's 10–6 record wasn't good enough to win the division or qualify for the postseason.

Seifert then proclaimed that if Montana was healthy, he would be the starter in 1992.

"It's insane," Young said. "I'm not going to accept number two status. It's illogical to go back."[105]

The 49ers didn't need a new helmet logo. They needed a federal quarterback mediator.

Young Wins the Job, Montana Makes a Curtain Call

BEFORE THE 1992 season, Mike Holmgren left his job as the 49ers' offensive coordinator when the Green Bay Packers hired him as head coach. This created concern back in the Bay. Over the previous five years, Holmgren had been the masterful buffer between Steve Young's impatience and Joe Montana's chronic insecurity, which dated back to his Notre Dame days.

Holmgren deserved a ton of credit. He had been Young's position coach at BYU before both came to the 49ers, where Holmgren renewed that relationship and built a new one with Montana. Young wanted to set the record straight, though.

"Everyone thinks that Mike's relationship with me was a certain way," Young said. "And we did get along great. But there were times I think it was like a father who is coaching his son on a Little League team. The guy is so conscious of not wanting to favor the kid, he goes too far the other way."[106]

With new offensive coordinator Mike Shanahan in place, Montana was eager to reclaim his starting job. But during summer camp, Montana's elbow again betrayed him. He needed two procedures to clean out scar tissue and relieve pressure on his ulnar nerve. He went back to the injured reserve list.

There Montana stayed, as Young helped his teammates roll to a 14–2 record and division title. He also topped the NFL in completion percentage (66.7), TD passes (25), and quarterback rating (107.0) and was named league MVP. His 537 rushing yards showed he hadn't lost a step. One opponent said playing against him was "60 minutes of hell."[107]

Even so, many fans were convinced Montana should take over when his elbow healed. With a playoff spot clinched, George Seifert announced that Montana would play the second half of Week 16 against Detroit at Candlestick.

The Bay Area quivered with joy and made the game appointment viewing. Montana took the field after halftime to a standing ovation in a horrible downpour, which meant Montana truly did have the opportunity to walk on water. He didn't. But he did do the next best thing: He was Joe. He drove the offense to three scores with two TD passes in a 24–6 victory. Clearly, he was no washed-up oldies act.

"It was my audition to go somewhere else," Montana said years later.[108]

Trivia question: Who caught Montana's last TD pass as a 49er? Answer: Amp Lee.

Steve Young took over as the 49ers quarterback and was the NFL MVP in 1992.

COURTESY OF MIKE POWELL/ALLSPORT/GETTY IMAGES

The San Francisco 49ers and Dallas Cowboys had an intense rivalry in the early 1990s.
COURTESY OF OTTO GREULE JR./ALLSPORT/GETTY IMAGES

The Dallas Doorstop, Nineties Version

IT'S FUNNY how what goes around comes around, especially with a star on its helmet. By 1992, the Dallas Cowboys had reclaimed their role as the 49ers' nemesis. In January 1993, the two teams met for the fourth time in the NFC Championship Game with a Super Bowl trip at stake.

Hype commenced. Joe Montana openly chafed at being Steve Young's backup for the game. Dallas touted its new stars—quarterback Troy Aikman, running back Emmitt Smith, and receiver Michael Irvin—as the next-generation 49er slayers. Charles Haley, the volatile defender who had caused locker room issues in San Francisco, had been traded to the Cowboys and was eager to unleash fury on his former team. Dallas legend Roger Staubach, Young's childhood hero and the one who broke 49er Faithful hearts in 1972, stood near the Cowboys' bench.

Rugged football also showed up. The halftime score was 10–10. Dallas's offense then took over, on the ground and in the air. The Niners' offense committed four turnovers. Aikman orchestrated a nine-minute drive to give the Cowboys a 24–13 lead early in the fourth quarter. With less than five minutes left, Young hit Jerry Rice for a touchdown to pull within 24–20. But Aikman struck back with a quick score to clinch a 30–20 decision.

At his locker, Young looked older than his 31 years, with welts on his forehead and a glazed expression. On a quarterback bootleg, a Dallas tackler had grabbed Young's helmet and it popped off, soaring through the air like a beach ball. With his unprotected head exposed to the world, Young still strained for yardage to set up a field goal. On the afternoon, he'd thrown for 313 yards and run for a touchdown. But he knew the deal. For demanding 49er fans, Young couldn't win unless he won it all. Would Montana have made a difference? Only if he had been able to play linebacker. Dallas controlled the scrimmage line and looked suspiciously like the better team all day.

Center Jesse Sapolu (left), quarterback Steve Young, and guard Harris Barton are stunned during the 1992 NFC Championship Game, which the 49ers lost to the Dallas Cowboys.

COURTESY OF MICHAEL ZAGARIS

"I really thought we were going to pull it out," Young said. "But Dallas came up with the big plays at the end, the way we have so many times over the years. Around here, we expect to go all the way . . . You know, you leave your heart and soul out there. I feel like I'm a walking shell right now."[109]

The Montana Exit Earthquake

CARMEN POLICY, the 49ers' team president, assessed the situation correctly. He said that trading away Joe Montana would be an "emotional earthquake" for the Bay Area.[110]

When it did indeed happen, the trade process also included a ride through a dizzy, fun-house roller coaster of confusion. Throughout the winter of 1992–93, Policy and coach George Seifert spent hours in discussions with Montana and his representatives about his future. Seifert made it clear that Steve Young was the No. 1 quarterback. Montana, whose contract ran for two more years, would enter the season as a backup. Montana didn't dig that idea. He received permission to explore other options.

Kansas City emerged as the best one. Policy cut a trade deal with the Chiefs that gave the 49ers a first-round pick. Montana wanted to break the news in person to owner Eddie DeBartolo, who was home in Ohio. Over Montana's 14 years with the team, the two had grown extremely close. When Montana flew back to Youngstown, both men grew teary-eyed. Eddie talked Joe into staying with the team. DeBartolo called Seifert to tell him Joe was again the No. 1 quarterback.

Seifert was taken aback. But he had to go along with his boss. The coach announced that Montana would be the "designated starter" for 1993. For one day, Joe's fans were ecstatic. By the next day, they were totally baffled. The caveat of Seifert's "decision" was that Montana had to play out his 49ers contract at $2.5 million per season. Kansas City had guaranteed him $8 million over two years. Montana decided to stick with his original choice and leave San Francisco. A farewell news conference was held on April 21 in Santa Clara. Montana was in a good mood and clearly relieved.

And where was Steve Young during all this? Hunkered down taking his law school exams in Utah, where he was studying in the offseason. "I got done with my last final," Young said, "I came out, and one of my friends called me: 'Did you hear? Joe was traded.' 'Really? I had no idea.' 'Yeah, it was a couple days ago!'"[111]

In the end, everybody got what they wanted. Montana had a lot more money and no quarterback controversy. The 49ers had a high draft pick to enhance their roster. Young was a firm No. 1. Of course, that "everybody" did not include Bay Area fans who felt they were personally connected to Montana through his 49er triumphs. They were crushed. They'd taken the ride with him as he became a local cultural icon. Now, he belonged to the Kansas City metropolitan area.

Joe Montana never looked comfortable watching from the sideline.
COURTESY OF PETER BROUILLET/GETTY IMAGES

Dallas Doorstop Redux

WITH THE quarterback soap opera finally over thanks to Joe Montana's exit, the 49ers set their sights on their one real mission: Getting back to the Super Bowl. Signs were promising in 1993. The offense led the NFL in scoring and yardage. Jerry Rice scored 15 touchdowns, and his 1,503 receiving yards topped the league.

In 1993, with no Montana in his rear-view mirror, Young became the first player in NFL history to win three consecutive passing titles. His 29 TD passes led the league, and his 4,023 yards passing also surpassed Montana's franchise record. More importantly, Young had won over the locker room. He had been presented the 1992 Len Eshmont Award, given to the 49ers' most inspirational and courageous player as voted on by his teammates.

After a 10–6 regular season, the Niners smothered the New York Giants 44–3 in their opening playoff game as Ricky Watters rushed for a playoff-record five touchdowns. This set up one more NFC Championship match-up with . . . as if anyone had any doubts . . . the déjà vu Dallas Cowboys.

The defending NFL champs had produced an impressive 12–4 regular season. They hosted the 49ers in Texas. Cowboys coach Jimmy Johnson was so confident that he guaranteed a victory.

Another pregame angle also excited the general public. Montana and the Kansas City Chiefs had reached the AFC title game. This raised the possibility of a Montana–Young matchup in the Super Bowl if both of their teams won.

Neither did. The Chiefs fell to Buffalo 30–13. The 49ers put up a slightly better fight. But with the score tied 7–7 in the second quarter, heavy pressure on Young caused him to overthrow John Taylor, whose fingertips deflected the ball to a Dallas defender. The Cowboys scored the next three touchdowns and took a 28–7 halftime lead, then cruised through the second half to win 38–21. Foiled by Dallas. Again.

Steve Young can't find answers against the Dallas defense in the 1993 NFC Championship Game.

COURTESY OF JAMES SMITH/GETTY IMAGES

September 5, 1994

Rice Reigns as Touchdown King

ONE SHOT. You get one shot. That was the word from the coaches' box upstairs. Jerry Rice would have just one more play to break Jim Brown's all-time NFL touchdown record on the stage where Rice most wanted to break it.

Belying his aw-shucks Mississippi exterior, Rice was a showoff at heart. As the September sun set at Candlestick Park and the 1994 Labor Day weekend came to a close, Rice realized that a huge audience would be viewing *Monday Night Football.* He came into the game at Candlestick Park needing two touchdowns to tie Brown's record of 126 career TDs, three to surpass it.

By early in the fourth quarter, Rice had scored twice. He'd matched Brown. But by then, the 49ers were leading the Los Angeles Raiders 37–14. With six minutes left, starters were being pulled. Rice did not want to be pulled. He wanted to go for history now. Right now. Just then, the Raiders turned over the ball on downs at their own 38-yard line.

The coaches gave Young and Rice one try for the record 127th touchdown.

On first down, Rice went in motion, right to left behind the line. With the snap, legs still moving, he took off directly upfield at full speed, bent the pattern slightly to his right and looked for the ball. Young, swarmed by the Raiders' rush, managed to get off the pass.

"Everybody in Candlestick knew that we would try to get the ball to Rice," said 49ers linebacker Gary Plummer. "Even the Raiders knew it."[112]

Rice was bracketed in coverage by two defensive backs as he crossed the 10-yard line. But this was your basic Jerry Rice screw-you-guys-don't-try-to-stop-me moment. He elevated above the defenders at the 2-yard line, reached up, and closed his hands on the ball. His momentum carried him into the end zone. Jerry Rice was the NFL's all-time touchdown leader.

Jerry Rice scores his record-setting 127th touchdown against Los Angeles Raiders defender Albert Lewis.

COURTESY OF JASON GROW/*SAN JOSE MERCURY NEWS*/MEDIANEWS GROUP VIA GETTY IMAGES

Rice's teammates lifted him to their shoulders. The crowd bellowed. "I can't think of a better evening," said Rice. "*Monday Night Football* and you've got everybody in the world watching. Plus, I really wanted it to be at home. What a day."[113]

By the time his career was done, Rice had scored 208 touchdowns. The one-shot, on-demand catch he summoned up that September night might have been his most cinematic.

Joe vs. Steve, Master vs. Student

WHEN THE 1994 NFL schedule was released, September 11 in Kansas City might as well have been circled in glowing, radioactive ink. A year after the Joe Montana trade, he and the Chiefs were set to face his old team and the man who took his job: Steve Young.

In retrospect, the Montana–Young relationship was far more complicated than a standard feud or rivalry. They had different personalities but were both decent guys. They didn't absolutely hate each other. They weren't pals, either, even if they sometimes played golf together and Montana once invited Young over for Thanksgiving dinner. Bill Walsh had simply put two of the most competitive people on earth into an impossible situation, believing it would bring out their best. George Seifert inherited the tension and never seemed sure how to handle it until Montana's move to the Chiefs put the whole thing to rest.

For one Sunday, however, the thing was alive again. Rightly or wrongly, fans saw it as a referendum on whether the 49ers should have let Montana go.

He and Young shook hands during pregame warmups and exchanged brief friendly words. They matched TD passes in the first half. The 49ers were up 14–7 when the Chiefs tackled Young in the end zone for a safety, making the halftime score 14–9. Young's offensive line was decimated by injuries to three starters. He was sacked four times and hammered after being chased out of the pocket. Montana's second TD pass and another conversion pass gave Kansas City a 17–14 lead. An attempted 49ers comeback ended when John Taylor fumbled after catching a Young pass.

The Chiefs prevailed 24–17. Montana completed 19 of 31 passes for 203 yards, two touchdowns, and no interceptions. Young completed 24 of 34 passes for 288 yards, a touchdown, and two interceptions. The two shook hands again afterward. Montana wished Young good luck and said he knew it was tough for Steve to lose a game "of this nature."

"This had a special meaning because it was my old team," Montana said. "But there's no feeling of vindication or anything. . . . I've got a lot of friends on that team."[114]

"Today the master had a little more to teach the student," Young said graciously.[115]

It hurt, though. Later that night, Young called his parents in Connecticut and left a phone message: "Joe's a hero, and I'm a schmuck."[116]

Joe Montana led the Kansas City Chiefs in a victory over his former team in 1994.

COURTESY OF STEPHEN DUNN/ALLSPORT/GETTY IMAGES

The Supporting Cast Takes Center Stage

A CONSISTENT FEATURE of the 49ers through the decades has been their ability to create star attractions. From Joe "The Jet" Perry to George "The People's Tight End" Kittle, the team's roster has included unforgettable characters. And more importantly, great football players. As of 2024, the Pro Football Hall of Fame has enshrined 30 former 49ers in Canton.

The 49ers of 1994 were particularly flush with standout names that fans came to know and love.

Ricky Watters led the pack in terms of flash. Drafted out of Notre Dame when Roger Craig left as a free agent, Watters rushed for 1,013 yards and had 405 receiving yards as a rookie in 1992, then followed it up with a combined 2,872 all-purpose yards and 22 touchdowns over the next two seasons. He also led the team in ego and arrogance before departing as a free agent in 1995.

Bryant Young, another Notre Dame alum, was the opposite of Watters in terms of self-importance but a mountain in terms of defensive line presence. He was named NFC Rookie of the Year in 1994, racking up six sacks and 49 tackles while making opposing offensive linemen miserable on the team's run to the Super Bowl. After multiple All-Pro seasons, his Canton induction was in 2022.

Brent Jones was a Bay Area native who had played wide receiver at Santa Clara University but bulked up to play tight end as a pro. He was drafted by Pittsburgh, but the Steelers cut him after a car accident injured his neck. The 49ers snapped him up, and all Jones did was make four Pro Bowls and catch 38 TD passes. No Niners tight end played more games (143) in his career. Jones' extroverted personality also made the locker room a more animated workplace.

Merton Hanks stepped into tough shoes as the 49ers' free safety after Ronnie Lott's departure and quickly earned his status as a fan favorite. His team-leading seven interceptions on the 1994 championship team helped, en route to 31 career pickoffs with the Niners. Hanks was often wrongly tabbed as the team's comic relief because he celebrated his big plays with a "Funky Chicken" strutting, jerky, neck-bobbing dance. In truth, Hanks was one of the more cerebral 49ers, filling up notebooks that tracked opponents' tendencies.

Of course, another 1994 roster addition hogged the prime attention.

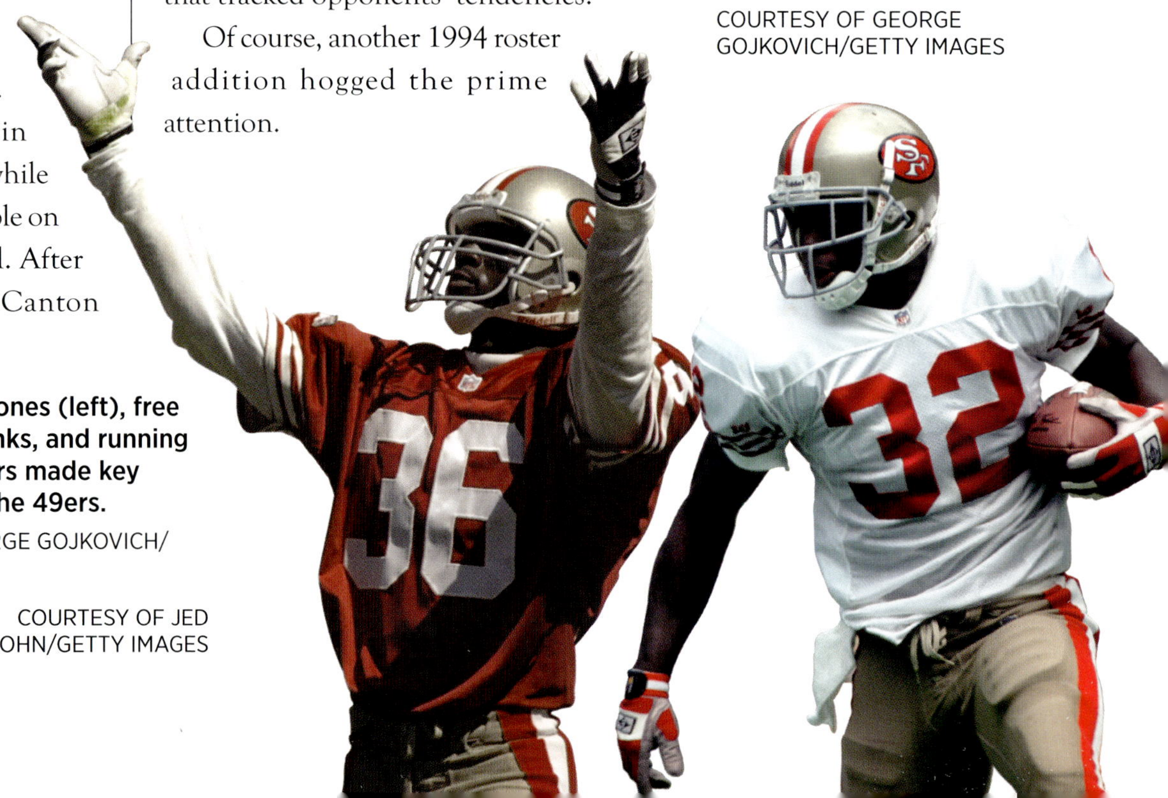

COURTESY OF GEORGE GOJKOVICH/GETTY IMAGES

Tight end Brent Jones (left), free safety Merton Hanks, and running back Ricky Watters made key contributions to the 49ers.

COURTESY OF GEORGE GOJKOVICH/ GETTY IMAGES

COURTESY OF JED JACOBSOHN/GETTY IMAGES

Cornerback Deion Sanders made an impact in his short stint with the 49ers.
COURTESY OF JOSEPH PATRONITE/GETTY IMAGES

1994

Prime-Time Deion Sanders

TWO PLAYOFF losses to the Cowboys had the 49ers' front office grasping for solutions. One was to steal linebacker Ken Norton Jr. away from Dallas as a free agent. Norton led the Niners in tackling while stabilizing the defensive middle.

The bigger spotlight shone on the 49ers' choice to recruit cornerback Deion Sanders, already famous for juggling an Atlanta Braves baseball career with an Atlanta Falcons football career. Looking to escape the Falcons' losing ways, Sanders put out word that he wanted to join an NFL winner. After a long free-agent courtship, the 49ers signed Sanders to a one-year, $1.1 million contract in mid-September, with the season already two games old. The man who modestly nicknamed himself "Prime Time" immediately lit up the 49ers' locker room with his officially licensed brashness.

"They've won four Super Bowls," Sanders said upon his arrival. "I'm here to make it five."[117]

And damned if he didn't. But first, during the regular season, he produced six interceptions, three of them pick-six touchdowns. In October, Sanders returned to Atlanta with the 49ers and delivered his most entertaining performance, featuring a slap fight with former teammate Andre Rison and a 93-yard interception return for a touchdown. As Sanders ran towards the Georgia Dome goal line, he stared down the Falcons bench, then high-stepped, stopped at the 1-yard line and strolled slowly into the end zone before breaking into a Deion dance.

After the 42–3 victory, Sanders let loose: "I've got one thing to say: This is my house! I built this and this is my house. I don't care if I'm with the Falcons or not. This is my house and this will always be my house."[118]

Reviews were mixed. Some of his 49er teammates enjoyed the act more than others. But they all respected Sanders' talent and energy. He was named NFL Defensive Player of the Year and contributed an end zone interception in the Super Bowl to help earn the ring he'd promised.

Eight months later, Sanders was playing for the Cowboys. Leveraging his one-year San Francisco cameo, he had negotiated a seven-year, $35 million deal. And he didn't even send the 49ers a thank-you note.

Running back Ricky Watters looks for room to run against the Dallas Cowboys in the 1994 NFC Championship Game. Both teams wore retro uniforms for the NFL's 75th anniversary.

COURTESY OF MIKE POWELL/GETTY IMAGES

January 15, 1995

No More Dallas Doorstop

DEPENDING ON how you like your alliteration, the 1994 Niners once more had to confront the Dallas Doorstop or the Cowboy Curse. For the third straight year, San Francisco and Dallas were the league's two best teams. But the 49ers had lost the two previous NFC title games to the Cowboys. Could San Francisco really write a different ending?

Never underestimate a team of motivated authors. Although the plot hit some potholes early in the season, such as an embarrassing 40–8 defeat at home to Philadelphia. In that one, George Seifert yanked Steve Young from the game in the third quarter following a violent sack. Young responded by pacing behind the bench and screaming angrily at Seifert's back, all captured on TV.

Young's uncharacteristic tantrum, counterintuitively, delighted his teammates. They loved seeing their quarterback show some fire. The 49ers proceeded to go on a 10-game winning streak and clinch the NFC West. In their playoff opener, they easily disposed of the Chicago Bears, 44–15. It set up Round 3 against their old Texas buddies.

Some things had changed in Dallas, however. Before the season, head coach Jimmy Johnson, choreographer of those previous big victories over the Niners, had resigned from the team after he and owner Jerry Jones had gotten sideways. Jones impulsively hired Barry Switzer, the former University of Oklahoma head coach. Barry was no Jimmy. During the Niners' win streak, they had defeated the Cowboys 21–14. That midseason victory firmed up the 49ers' confidence that Dallas could be conquered in the NFC title game.

The Cowboys' first drive was cut short when Eric Davis returned an interception 44 yards for a touchdown. The next two Dallas possessions ended in fumbles, setting up two quick San Francisco scores for a 21–0 lead in the game's first eight minutes.

The 49ers did not maintain that one-touchdown-every-160-seconds pace. But they kept the Cowboys at bay in a brutal battle. A three-yard TD run by Young locked up a 38–28 victory. The Dallas Doorstop was gone. The Cowboys Curse, ditto. Young celebrated by taking a lap around Candlestick and high-fiving fans chanting his name. Young knew some were the same fans who had booed him for not being Joe Montana. Didn't matter. "It was as if everyone's heart grew enough to circle both of us," Young said poetically, with one more happy chapter to write.[119]

Quarterback Steve Young stretches to finally clear the hurdle against the Dallas Cowboys in the 1994 NFC Championship Game.

COURTESY OF JOHN G. MABANGLO/AFP VIA GETTY IMAGES

The 49ers stifle San Diego Chargers running back Natrone Means during Super Bowl XXIX.
COURTESY OF JONATHAN DANIEL/ALLSPORT/GETTY IMAGES

Super Bowl XXIX: Focused on the End Prize

THERE WERE abundant reasons to doubt that the San Diego Chargers might pose a real challenge to the 49ers in Super Bowl XXIX. The NFC had won the 10 previous matchups against the AFC. Bookmakers had made San Diego an 18.5-point underdog. The 49ers' impressive takedown of Dallas for the NFC title had seemed to settle the issue of which team was the league's best. Super Bowl? Who needed the Super Bowl?

Still, the game had to be played. Niners head coach George Seifert was under extra pressure to produce another Super Bowl title. The 1989 championship team during his first season as head coach was largely viewed as a carryover from the Bill Walsh era. Seifert, at that point, had won almost 80 percent of his games as an NFL head coach and owned an 8–3 mark in playoff games. But in San Francisco, Lombardi Trophies were expected every year.

Just like his quarterback, Seifert had been saddled with replacing a future Hall of Famer. Not an easy gig. Seifert had carried the burden with good humor. Earlier in the season, the team's 32-point loss to the Eagles had prompted a San Francisco radio station to conduct a call-in poll asking if Seifert should be fired. Of the 700 people who phoned in, 85 percent were in favor of dumping him. Asked for a reaction, Seifert deadpanned: "Well, I'd like to thank the 15 percent who voted for me."[120]

The circus of Super Bowl media week fomented wild speculation of whether Seifert would be fired if the 49ers lost. Or if Jerry Rice had said this would his "last Super Bowl" and that he might retire, all based on an out-of-context quote. Rice's full statement was: "It's so hard to get back to the Super Bowl now and it took us five years to get back, so I'm looking at this game as my last Super Bowl so I can be focused."[121]

The football world soon discovered exactly how focused the 49ers were.

Jerry Rice catches a pass behind Junior Seau of the Chargers.
COURTESY OFJOSEPH PATRONITE/GETTY IMAGES

Ricky Watters stiff-arms Chargers linebacker David Griggs during Super Bowl XXIX.
COURTESY OF RICK STEWART/GETTY IMAGE

January 29, 1995

Super Bowl XXIX: Getting the Monkey Off Their Back

THE 49ERS took the field on an 81-degree Florida night at Joe Robbie Stadium in Miami wearing their throwback red jerseys with the shadowed numerals. Then they blacked out the San Diego Chargers.

So much for worries that the Niners might come up flat after their emotional victory over Dallas two weeks earlier. As it turned out, quarterback Steve Young and offensive coordinator Mike Shanahan had spent extra hours cooking up special new looks and plays to confuse and melt down the San Diego defense.

"Mike and I wanted to make a statement about the 49ers," Young said later. "Yeah, we've been to the Super Bowl before. But you've never seen *this* one before."[122]

It definitely looked that way. On the third play from scrimmage, Young faked a handoff to fullback William Floyd and sent a deep ball to Jerry Rice, who split two defenders for a 44-yard touchdown. Four minutes later, Young hit Ricky Watters at the 35-yard line and Watters broke two tackles on the way to the end zone. Less than five minutes had elapsed. The 49ers were already up by 14 points.

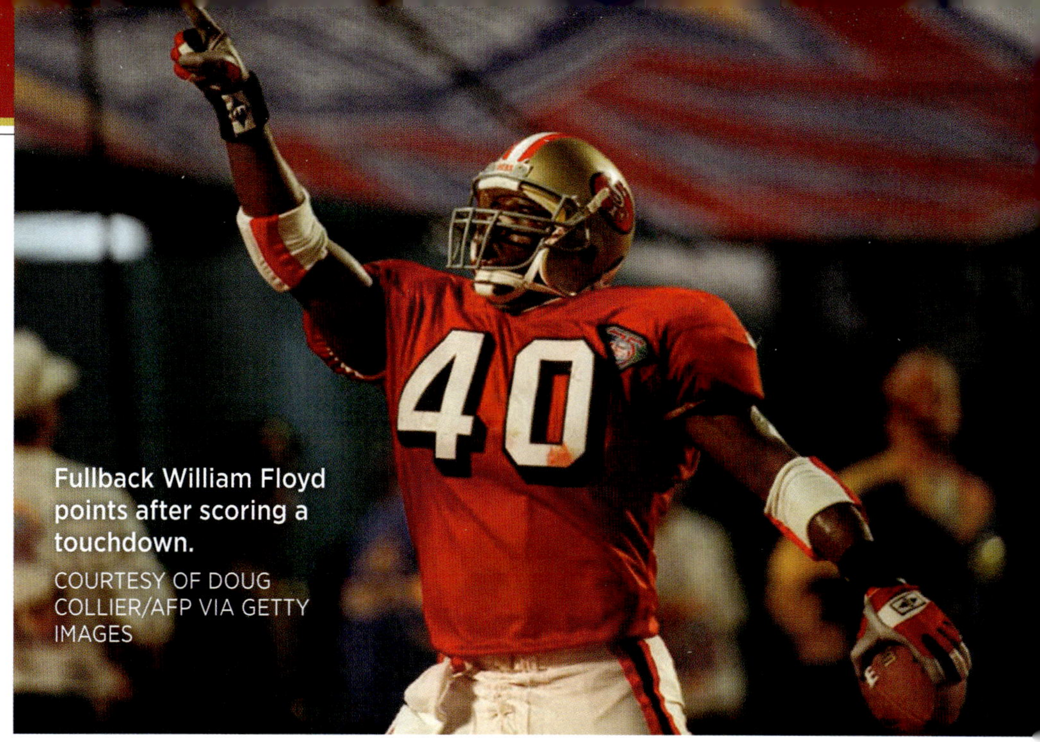

Fullback William Floyd points after scoring a touchdown.

COURTESY OF DOUG COLLIER/AFP VIA GETTY IMAGES

By halftime, the score was 28–10. By the fourth quarter, the 49ers were ahead 42–18 and Young had thrown five TD passes. He made it six with a slant pass to Rice. It broke the previous record of five TDs that Joe Montana had set in Super Bowl XXIV.

Steve Young and Jerry Rice celebrate Young's fifth touchdown pass of Super Bowl XXIX.

COURTESY OF JEFF HAYNES/AFP VIA GETTY IMAGES

Young then spent the final minutes of the 49–26 crush job on the sidelines in a baseball cap. As the clock wound down, Young was giddily pacing in front of the 49ers' bench. Reveling in the moment, he shouted: "Someone take the monkey off my back, please!" Teammates Gary Plummer and Steve Wallace reached onto Young's shoulders and tugged off an invisible, imaginary simian.

Over the years, Young has said he regretted that moment because he didn't realize the cameras were there and because it didn't capture his true feelings. He would insist that the challenge of following Montana was an incentive and inspiration, not an encumbrance.

"Rather than just relief and 'Great to get this weight off me,' it was really, truly another piece to the puzzle in finding really how good I can be with this team," Young said.[123]

A few months later, on April 18, 1995, Joe Montana returned to San Francisco and announced his retirement from football at the waterfront Justin Herman Plaza in front of 25,000 Bay Area fans.

Packers Become the New Roadblock, So Mooch Moves In

NO ONE was taking victory laps around Candlestick Park after the 1995 or 1996 seasons, both of which ended in playoff losses to Green Bay. The 49ers' front office was still adjusting to the tricky little salary cap curve that the NFL had thrown at them and the rest of the league—principally because of the way 49ers owner Eddie DeBartolo spent whatever it took to put the best team on the field. Other franchises were more budget conscious. A mandated lid on league payrolls was the result, starting in 1994.

A juggling act began in the executive offices. Carmen Policy sought creative ways to keep as much talent as possible. But creativity went only so far. The Niners lost Ricky Watters, Deion Sanders, and others to free agency before the 1995 season. When injuries struck, that mattered.

In Week 7, Steve Young's shoulder was wrenched out of whack in a loss to the Indianapolis Colts. The entire season seemed in jeopardy. An MRI revealed a partially torn rotator cuff and deep bone bruise. Young was out indefinitely. Backup quarterback Elvis Grbac was plugged into the lineup.

Surprise of surprises, Elvis rocked. He held down the fort and helped upset the Cowboys in Week 11. Jerry Rice set records with 122 receptions and 1,848 receiving yards that season. Then Young returned for the final stretch, finishing off a five-game winning streak to enter the playoffs with some swagger. "This is December," Rice said after the division clincher. "This is when we win games."[124]

Unfortunately, their first postseason game was played in January—against Green Bay, coached by the Niners' former offensive coordinator, Mike Holmgren. His game plan undid and upset the Niners 27–17. After the 49ers' 12-win season in 1996, the Packers and quarterback Brett Favre pulled off a repeat with a statement 35–14 playoff victory over the 49ers at Lambeau Field. Young missed most of the game with injured ribs.

The Packers were now officially the 49ers' roadblock. DeBartolo and Policy responded with a shocker. They had grown enamored of Steve "Mooch" Mariucci, the ebullient head coach of Cal's football team across the Bay. They offered him a job as the 49ers' offensive coordinator for the 1997 season with a guarantee of ascending to the head coaching job in 1998. George Seifert refused to stamp an expiration date on his forehead and resigned. The Mooch era was underway.

Muddy quarterbacks Steve Young and Brett Favre chat after the Green Bay Packers won another playoff game over the 49ers in January 1998.

COURTESY OF MICKEY PFLEGER/GETTY IMAGES

NFC WEST DIVISION 1995-2001

- ATLANTA FALCONS
- CAROLINA PANTHERS
- NEW ORLEANS SAINTS
- ST. LOUIS RAMS
- SAN FRANCISCO 49ERS

Mariucci's Rough Start, Rice's Miraculous Return

STEVE MARIUCCI could not have asked for a more harrowing debut as the 49ers' new head coach. In the 1997 season opener at Tampa Bay, Steve Young suffered a concussion. Minutes later, franchise icon Jerry Rice ran an end-around play and was tackled by his face mask, which Tampa defender Warren Sapp twisted in a clockwise direction. Rice's left foot was planted firmly in the turf, causing his knee to spin in a counterclockwise direction. Rice fell to the turf, holding his leg. Sapp was penalized. Rice was in anguish.

After playing in 189 consecutive games, Rice now needed surgery for a torn anterior cruciate ligament. He was out for the year, supposedly. Rice had different ideas. He pledged to return before the end of the season. But what would the 49ers and their new coach do without him?

Win and win and win. Somehow, over three months, Coach Mooch transformed himself from an unproven NFL student driver into pro football's version of a NASCAR points leader. He maneuvered his team into an 11-game victory streak. Young's quick return to action helped. So did running back Garrison Hearst's 1,019 rushing yards. But the 49ers' defense did the heavy lifting, boosted by the addition of Rod Woodson and Kevin Greene to the regular lineup of Pro Bowlers like Ken Norton Jr., Dana Stubblefield, Bryant Young, Tim McDonald, and Lee Woodall.

As an added miracle attraction, Rice did indeed fulfill his promise to rehab his knee aggressively and suited up for the December 15 Monday night game at which Joe Montana's No. 16 jersey was retired. In the first half of a 34–17 subjugation of the Denver Broncos, Rice made a diving 14-yard TD catch. Candlestick went bonkers. "I don't think in my five years here, I've ever heard a crowd that loud," McDonald said.[125]

But Rice had trouble getting up from the end zone catch. He had landed hard and cracked his left kneecap, which was weakened by the surgery. This time, Rice really was done for the year.

A month later, so were the Niners. After their stellar 13–3 regular season and a 38–22 thumping of Minnesota, San Francisco again faced Green Bay in the NFC Championship Game. An injury to Hearst left the 49ers offense painfully one-dimensional. The Packers cleaned up all the other dimensions in their 23–10 victory.

Defying the odds, Jerry Rice returned from a torn ACL and MCL after just 14 weeks.

COURTESY OF JOHN G. MABANGLO/AFP VIA GETTY IMAGES

Steve Mariucci had a rude awakening in his first game as the 49ers' heads coach.

COURTESY OF ANDY LYONS/ GETTY IMAGES

Garrison Hearst's 96-yard touchdown run in overtime beat the New York Jets in the 1998 opener.
COURTESY OF OTTO GREULE JR./ALLSPORT/GETTY IMAGES

Hearst's 96-Yard Run Electrifies the Stick

THE 49ERS of 1998 sprinkled their 12–4 season in 1998 with extremely watchable highlights. Opening day in September provided the most fabulous one, featuring running back Garrison Hearst as the 96-yard man. He won a sudden-death overtime game against the New York Jets, 36–30, by taking the football and running a complete lap around the Bay Area before reaching the end zone.

Felt like it, anyway. With the 49ers backed up at their own 4-yard line, Hearst charged through the hole created by his blockers, stopped at Pier 39 for lunch, put a straight-arm into one defender, slashed across the bridge to Oakland for coffee, cut back and hit a drive-thru burger window in San Jose, then rumbled the last few steps toward the goal line.

And scored. Game over. Ninety. Six. Yards.

"That," said Steve Mariucci, "will go down in history as one of the great, great runs of all time."[126]

It was also the longest run in 49ers history. The previous team record of 89 yards had been set by Hugh McElhenny in 1952. By the clock, Hearst's journey down the field lasted 17 seconds. It unfurled like a three-part miniseries. The actual play-by-play: Hearst charged through the trap blocking at the line of scrimmage, weaved to the right sideline, broke five tackles along the way, then gulped for air as he carried a Jets linebacker across the goal line.

"Really, I was just looking for 3 yards on that play," Hearst claimed. "But I saw our blockers take out the defensive lineman and I said to myself, 'Hey, we've got a chance here.'"[127]

Steve Young had a hard act to follow in the next 15 weeks. But the 37-year-old quarterback had one of his best seasons. He again led the league with 36 passing touchdowns and threw for 300-plus yards in six consecutive games to set an NFL record. In October, he rallied the 49ers from a 21-point deficit by running for two touchdowns and passing for two others to beat Indianapolis and rookie quarterback Peyton Manning, 34–31. The signature moment was Young's 23-yard TD run in the fourth quarter when he powered through two Colts tacklers for a touchdown.

"He does it all," said 49ers fullback Marc Edwards with admiration. "Who knows? We might put him back to return kicks."[128]

Steve Young threw for his career-best yardage and touchdowns in 1998.

COURTESY OF KIRBY LEE/GETTY IMAGES

Eddie D's Louisiana Debacle and Canton Comeback

THE PERFECT marriage between Eddie DeBartolo and his beloved 49ers was broken up by a riverboat casino. Or to be exact, DeBartolo's pursuit of a riverboat casino. The pursuit culminated in a franchise meltdown and shakeup at the ownership and executive levels.

Denise DeBartolo York took over ownership of the 49ers from her brother, Eddie DeBartolo.

COURTESY OF MICHAEL MACOR/ *THE SAN FRANCISCO CHRONICLE* VIA GETTY IMAGES

In 1996, DeBartolo wanted to expand his family's holdings in Louisiana, where it already owned a racetrack. The state was getting into legalized gambling. Former governor Edwin Edwards promised DeBartolo he could secure one of the treasured casino licenses—with a sleazy caveat. Edwards asked DeBartolo for a briefcase full of $400,000 in $100 bills. The FBI used wiretaps and hidden microphones to expose the scheme. DeBartolo obtained the license. But he dropped the riverboat project after being subpoenaed to testify before a grand jury that was investigating the deal.

That set off the turmoil. When word surfaced in 1997 of the federal probe and of DeBartolo's involvement, the 49ers were caught in the backwash. The NFL discussed a suspension. DeBartolo announced that he would take no active role with the team until the case was resolved. The situation festered for more than a year—and grew uglier by the month.

Eddie's sister, Denise DeBartolo York, and her husband, John York, were initially reluctant to step into the breach. They allowed team president and general manager Carmen Policy to keep running the team—until Policy angered the whole family by clandestinely assembling a potential ownership group to buy the 49ers in case Eddie was arrested and forced to sell.

Not cool. Out the door went Policy. In the door came DeBartolo Corporation attorney Larry Thrailkill, who had no pro football experience and suddenly found himself as the caretaker CEO of a legacy NFL franchise.

In October 1998, Eddie DeBartolo pled guilty in Louisiana for failing to report a bribe. He was given two years' probation, ordered to pay $1 million in fines, and was required to testify against Edwards. Based partially on DeBartolo's testimony, Edwards was found guilty of racketeering and extortion. He served a nine-year prison sentence.

Meanwhile, Denise and John York sold DeBartolo's private jet and asked him to reimburse certain expenses. Eddie fumed. Lawsuits were filed. End result: DeBartolo surrendered ownership of the 49ers. The Yorks ended up in full control of the team.

By 2016, Eddie DeBartolo had put Louisiana behind him and, based on his five Lombardi trophies plus the way he raised the standards for NFL franchises' treatment of players, was elected to the Pro Football Hall of Fame. In 2020, he was given a presidential pardon. Time heals some wounds.

The 49ers' owner, Eddie DeBartolo, got into legal troubles and was forced to give up the team.

COURTESY OF OTTO GREULE JR./ GETTY IMAGES

"The Catch II" and the Birth of T.O.

THE 1998 postseason produced another episode of that popular NFL docudrama, Niners vs. Their Personal Green Demons. Yes, the Packers. The same Green Bay outfit that had won five straight games against the 49ers. Including three playoff eliminations. This time, it would be different. And the emotion would be off the charts.

In the playoff opener at Candlestick Park, the two teams went back and forth sloppily for nearly four quarters, neither leading the other by more than a touchdown. Players bobbled passes, lost fumbles, and overcame multiple interceptions by both Steve Young and the Packers' Brett Favre to set up the finish.

And heavens to Vince Lombardi, what a finish. After Favre had given the Packers a 27–23 lead on a TD pass to Antonio Freeman with two minutes remaining, the 49ers drove downfield to the Green Bay 25-yard line. Eight seconds left. No timeouts. The play call was "All Go." A schoolyard play, more or less.

Young took the snap and nearly stumbled as he dropped back. But he raised his head in time to see a glorious hole in the Green Bay coverage. There. Right there. At the goal line. It was Terrell Owens, who had dropped four passes earlier in the game. He bent his "All Go" route slightly left to the open spot, splitting two Green Bay defenders. Young placed the ball perfectly into Owens' arms.

Defensive backs Darren Sharper and Pat Terrell sandwiched the 49er receiver with simultaneous vicious hits to try and jar the ball loose. Owens didn't lose his grip on this one. Niners 30, Packers 27. Green Demons vanquished.

"I was just happy I caught the ball," said Owens, who streamed tears as the Candlestick noise washed over him. "I had a rough day up to that point. All year, I'd been making plays. I didn't want to get into a big game and choke up. I'm glad I got the chance to redeem myself. This was a perfect ending."[129]

San Francisco wide receiver Terrell Owens hauls in the game-winning touchdown pass with seconds left against the Green Bay Packers.

COURTESY OF BRUCE GORDON/
AFP VIA GETTY IMAGES

To the game, yes. But the season did not end perfectly. Six days later, the 49ers lost at Atlanta 20–18 after Garrison Hearst broke his leg on the first offensive play. The literal bad break ruined any Super Bowl hopes. But the Green Bay victory made the offseason easier to take. Owens' touchdown—dubbed "The Catch II"—was a turning point in his career. The previously shy kid from Alabama found that he enjoyed the attention. He began morphing into the flamboyant "T.O." He would be heard from again.

A new generation of 49ers players filled the roster in the 2000s. From left: Matt Willig, Jeff Garcia, J. J. Stokes, Ray Brown, Terrell Owens, Jeremy Newberry, Tai Streets, and Dave Fiore.
COURTESY OF DAVID MADISON/GETTY IMAGES

CHAPTER 5 THE GOLD, THE BAD, AND THE UGLY 1999–2016

A QUESTION LOOMED. What would the 49ers franchise look like without Eddie DeBartolo in the owners' office, demanding Super Bowls or else? After the 1998 playoff loss, Steve Mariucci was asked who would lead the 49ers in the next year. "We'll get it all worked out and have people in the right places," assured Mariucci, perhaps the only time a coach had to give a vote of confidence to team management, not vice versa.[130]

The DeBartolo/York family stabilized the front office by asking Bill Walsh to return as general manager. But after two seasons, he yielded the job to hand-picked successor Terry Donahue. And after Steve Young's retirement following a severe concussion, the team fell into a nine-year losing trench with four different head coaches.

In 2010, Jed York assumed the CEO role. In a daring move, he hired Stanford coach Jim Harbaugh, who steered the team to another Super Bowl but failed to close the deal, while giving the NFL its most politically demonstrative quarterback in history. No matter the era, the 49ers couldn't avoid being an attention-grabbing franchise. > > >

Steve Young's Concussion, Jeff Garcia's Ascension

STEVE YOUNG was not going to quarterback the 49ers forever. But the way his exit played out was a sudden shock. In a Week 3 game at Arizona on a Monday night in 1999, Young was hit by two blitzing defensive backs, one high and one low. As he toppled backward, his helmet struck the knee of a 49er lineman. When Young hit the turf, he blacked out. He regained consciousness but left the field and didn't return.

It would be the last play of his football career.

Change happens abruptly and cruelly in the NFL. The unexpected torch-pass from Young to Jeff Garcia was a classic example.

General manager Bill Walsh had signed Garcia as a free agent out of the Canadian Football League, after he had quarterbacked the Calgary Stampeders to a Grey Cup championship. But Garcia was a Bay Area guy, from Gilroy High School and San Jose State, where Walsh had first spotted him. After going undrafted by the NFL, Garcia rose to stardom in Calgary.

"I could have stayed in Canada and been comfortable," Garcia said upon his arrival at the 49ers summer camp. "But I've worked every year in football to get this kind of opportunity. And finally it's here. I believe I can come in and compete for that No. 2 job, and that's all I can ask."[131]

After Young's injury, the 49ers asked him to do a lot more. Garcia won his first start with two TD passes and one TD run, then struggled along with the team through an ugly 4–12 season laced with injuries and bad vibes. But the raps against Garcia's arm strength and size—6-foot-1, 195 pounds—were misplaced. His arm was fine. His mobility bought him pocket time. He was unafraid to scramble for a first down. And he loved playing in front of friends and family.

"It's definitely a dream come true," Garcia said. "And the dream will continue."[132]

Young, after digesting medical opinions from his new wife, announced his retirement at an emotional news conference in June 2000. The 49ers, who had been lucky enough to employ two future Hall of Fame quarterbacks back-to-back, were entering new territory with the guy from Gilroy.

Jeff Garcia took over as quarterback in 1999 after Steve Young's injury, then stayed as the No. 1 starter.
COURTESY OF MATT A. BROWN/ICON SPORTSWIRE VIA GETTY IMAGES

After 16 seasons with the 49ers, Jerry Rice said farewell in 2000.
COURTESY OF JED JACOBSOHN/ALLSPORT /GETTY IMAGES

December 17, 2000

Rice's Party Doubled as the T.O. Show

NEAR THE end of the 2000 season, the 49ers threw a warm and wonderful farewell party for Jerry Rice. He didn't receive a gold watch. Instead, he was allowed to leave San Francisco as a free agent, which was his choice. He also took a final San Francisco bow on an emotional night where Terrell Owens provided added entertainment.

The boisterous Candlestick Park crowd loved all of it. In Rice's last home game with the Niners, a 17–0 victory over the Chicago Bears, he caught his share of passes for 76 yards. But the most sensational numbers were provided by his younger sidekick, Owens. The Bears tried to spoil Rice's day by smothering him with double coverage. This left Owens consistently wide open. He broke a 50-year-old NFL record by accumulating 20 receptions for 283 yards and a touchdown.

"What I did by no means overshadows No. 80," said Owens. "He's been very instrumental in my success. He taught me a lot on and off the field. And definitely, if you want to say that torch has been passed, I'll just take that torch and keep going."[133]

"I was happy for him," Rice said of Owens. "I was the first one to congratulate him. He had the ultimate day."[134]

They were classy words from the man who had the ultimate 49er career, which concluded as a necessary evil. Bill Walsh's comeback stint as general manager lasted two brief seasons. But his toughest personnel decision involved Rice. At age 38, Rice was nearing the end of his contract. He wanted to keep playing. Walsh looked at the books. The 49ers were a projected $11 million over the salary cap for 2001. Walsh knew he had to shed Rice, whom he called "the last significant player from a bygone era of true greatness with this organization."[135] When Walsh broke the news to Rice, he understood. "No animosity," Rice said. "I've had a great career here."[136]

With 16 seconds remaining in his final game in red and gold, Rice ran a hook pattern for a 24-yard gain as the crowd erupted. He jogged off the field, high-fived Owens, and hugged coaches and teammates. Rice took a victory lap around the stadium, slapping the hands of fans before climbing a midfield stage to speak.

"Guys," Rice said, tears streaming down his face, "I think it's time for me to go. But San Francisco, I'll always love you guys."[137]

Wide receiver Terrell Owens celebrating on the Dallas star began a pattern of showboating that ruffled 49ers coach Steve Mariucci.

COURTESY OF BRIAN BAHR/GETTY IMAGES

2002

The Terrell Owens Troubles

NFC WEST DIVISION 2002–PRESENT

- ARIZONA CARDINALS
- LOS ANGELES/ST. LOUIS RAMS
- SAN FRANCISCO 49ERS
- SEATTLE SEAHAWKS

HOW DO you solve a problem like Terrell Owens? The 49ers tried for eight seasons. They never did figure it out. Owens's talent and skills as a wide receiver were striking and undeniable. His attitude and extracurricular antics were exasperating. Entertaining, yes. But exasperating. As he transformed from "Terrell" into "T.O.," Owens challenged his coaches with theatrical behavior that led to suspensions and arguments.

His first attention-grabbing stunt took place in a 41–24 victory at Dallas in 2000. He celebrated two touchdowns by sprinting from the end zone to the Cowboys' large star logo at midfield, then posing with his arms outstretched as the crowd booed. The second time Owens did it, Dallas safety George Teague followed Owens and star-slammed him, sparking a scuffle between the teams. Niners coach Steve Mariucci suspended Owens for a week. Owens didn't care.

COURTESY OF *THE SPORTING NEWS* VIA GETTY IMAGES

"I don't regret what I was doing," he said. "I bring my own emotion to the game, and I can't let him take away from my game."[138]

Owens accused Mariucci of blowing a 17-point lead to the Bears in 2001, saying that Mooch had taken his foot off the gas because he was friends with the Chicago coach. Mariucci said Owens' accusation was "utterly ridiculous" and "void of any deep thought."[139] Their glacial relationship continued, as did the stunts.

After scoring a touchdown in a 2002 Monday night game in Seattle, Owens pulled a Sharpie pen out of his sock and autographed the football, then walked over to a luxury suite and handed the ball to his financial advisor. Jeff Garcia and T.O. also had an up-and-down relationship.

Little wonder that Owens had few 49er friends, even as some veteran players felt empathy for him because of his background. As a poor kid growing up in Alabama, Owens didn't learn until he was a teenager that his father was living across the street and wanted nothing to do with him. The 49er vets saw the insecurity behind the bluster. The T.O. act jumped from San Francisco to Philadelphia to Dallas to Buffalo to Cincinnati before his career ended.

In 2018, when he was elected to the Hall of Fame, Owens boycotted the ceremony in Canton, Ohio, and staged his own private "induction" at his college's basketball arena. It was one last T.O. football stunt.

Wide receiver Tai Streets scores the winning touchdown in the 49ers' epic comeback win over the New York Giants in the 2002 NFC Wild Card playoff game.
COURTESY OF JOHN G. MABANGLO/AFP VIA GETTY IMAGES

The Most Giant 49ers Comeback Ever

BETWEEN 1999 and 2010, the 49ers produced a single playoff victory. But it was one heck of a raucous wild ride of a game. After winning the NFC West in 2002, the Niners hosted a first-round game against the New York Giants, who rolled into San Francisco and rolled out to a big lead. With 4:27 left in the third quarter, the 49ers trailed 38–14.

The giant sucking sound in the air was not just the season going down the commode. It was the sound of life being drained out of Candlestick Park.

"Things weren't necessarily going in the direction we wanted them to go," said Jeff Garcia.[140]

Uh, no. They were not. Steve Mariucci was desperate. The 49ers' coach turned loose the team's two-minute, no-huddle offense. And it worked. The Niners scored, and scored again, and again and again. After Terrell Owens caught a touchdown, Giants defensive end Michael Strahan taunted him by pointing to the scoreboard. Big mistake. The Niners responded with TDs by Garcia and Tai Streets as they stormed from behind to win, 39–38. Candlestick became a ridiculous, soaring, bleating Burning Man football festival.

"Once we got 20 points on the board and made our first two-point conversion, they were back on their heels a little bit," Owens said.[141]

Overcoming a 24-point deficit was the NFL's second-largest playoff comeback ever. In the postgame locker room, Mariucci gave his trenchant, detailed analysis of the victory: "Wow."[142]

In fairness, the 49ers also got a little lucky. The game ended when the Giants botched a 41-yard field goal attempt as time expired. The long snapper skidded the ball across the ground to holder Matt Allen, who scooped it up, scrambled, then lofted a pass toward teammate Rich Seubert at the goal line. Seubert was hauled down by 49er defender Chike Okeafor. It looked like pass interference. But officials ruled that New York had ineligible linemen downfield. So, the game was whistled over. Incorrectly, as it turned out. The next day, the NFL said that a penalty should have been called on Okeafor, which would have meant offsetting penalties, with the down played over. But it was too late to nullify the result—or the memorable Candlestick frenzy.

"I wish I could have bottled up the feeling in the stands," Garcia said. "That feeling in the stadium is hard to match any other feeling I've had in my life."[143]

Quarterback Jeff Garcia shouts after running in a touchdown against the New York Giants.
COURTESY OF MONICA DAVEY/AFP VIA GETTY IMAGES

Mariucci's Firing Starts a Downward Spiral

HEAD COACHING jobs in the NFL are like solar eclipses. Rare and not permanent. The men who take those jobs understand this scientific fact. Nevertheless, when Steve Mariucci was fired as the 49ers' head coach three days after a 31–6 playoff loss to Tampa Bay in January 2003, he was as surprised as anyone other than team owner John York.

Mariucci's 49ers contract had one more year to run. Given his 22–10 record over the previous two seasons, he was hoping an extension might include more control over certain aspects of the football operations. This conflicted with the desires of general manager Terry Donahue, who had cultivated a strong relationship with York. Confronted with that choice, York told Mariucci he would no longer be the team's head coach. Adios, Mooch.

His departure marked the start of a downward coaching spiral. Donahue replaced Mariucci with Dennis Erickson, who had plenty of experience winning at the college and pro level but went 9–23 over two seasons with the Niners. He was sacked and succeeded by Mike Nolan, son of former Niners' coach Dick Nolan. It made for a great story but lousy football. Nolan won just 18 of 55 games before he was terminated mid-season in 2008 and supplanted by his assistant, Mike Singletary. The former Chicago Bears linebacker won eight of his first 13 games and made headlines by dropping his pants during a locker room pep talk to illustrate some point or other. The tactic failed. Singletary lost 17 of his last 27 games and was gone after the 2010 season.

The unstable leadership wasted some show-bizzy talent. Wide receiver Brandon Lloyd was a sporadic but sensational highlight reel with a repertoire of leaping, one-handed magic tricks. Offensive tackle Joe Staley, drafted out of Central Michigan, persevered through the tough years and reached the Pro Bowl six times. Justin Smith came aboard as a free agent and gave the 49ers a professional example of how to excel on the defensive line amidst turbulence. There was lots of that.

Even during lean years, the 49ers had dynamic players like Brandon Lloyd, who was known for acrobatic one-handed catches.

COURTESY OF NHAT V. MEYER/ MEDIANEWS GROUP/BAY AREA NEWS VIA GETTY IMAGES

A Series of Unfortunate Alex Smith Events

ALEX SMITH was only 20 years old on the night of the 2005 NFL draft, when the 49ers made him the No. 1 overall pick out of Utah. In hindsight, it's bizarre to think that the 49ers installed him as their starting quarterback as a rookie. But they did. During his eight years with the team, they also saddled Smith with four different head coaches and seven different offensive coordinators.

It was a recipe for failure, and Smith deserved better. His situation was created by a perfect storm of bad circumstances.

The salary cap monster had finally devoured the 49ers in the 2000s. After the cap was instituted in 1994, general manager Carmen Policy figured out tricks, such as huge up-front bonuses and stretched-out deals, to manipulate the system. This kept their roster very competitive over the cap's first five years. But the tricks ran out. Loopholes were closed. The cap monster could not be tamed.

In 2004, the 49ers released Jeff Garcia, whose underrated 49er career included four Pro Bowls. The team used journeymen Tim Rattay and Ken Dorsey as alternating quarterbacks during an unwatchable 2–14 season. The Niners needed someone in the 2005 draft who could play right away.

Back in 2000, they could have drafted Tom Brady, who played high school football in the Bay Area, but instead picked quarterback Giovanni Carmazzi, who played zero NFL downs. Brady won seven Super Bowls.

Then came the draft decision that 49er fans will debate forever. Coach Mike Nolan chose Alex Smith over Aaron Rodgers of Cal in nearby Berkeley. After he was chosen by Green Bay, a reporter asked how disappointed Rodgers was that the 49ers hadn't drafted him. "Not as disappointed as the 49ers will be that they didn't draft *me*," he said.[144]

Who knows what would have happened if Rodgers had been thrust into the same situation as Smith? Nolan waited only five weeks before giving Smith his first starting assignment, against Peyton Manning and the Indianapolis Colts. Smith threw four interceptions, lost a fumble, and was sacked five times in a 28–3 defeat.

Alex Smith, the 49ers' No. 1 draft pick in 2005, struggled with a carousel of coaches for several years.
COURTESY OF EZRA SHAW/GETTY IMAGES

In his first five seasons, Smith went 19–31 as a starter with more interceptions (53) than TD passes (51). He was revitalized when Jim Harbaugh showed up in 2011 to provide better coaching. And the 49ers started winning.

Frank Gore, Earnest Rushing Hero

THE MOST vivid memory of Frank Gore, for anyone who saw the running back in locker rooms after 49er games, is of a man covered in ice bags. During a stretch of seasons when the team had little offense, Gore was frequently the entire game plan. He would carry the ball 20 or 25 times and then limp into his postgame interviews with frozen packs all over his body, refrigerating his pain.

And so it was late one afternoon in 2006. On this specific Sunday, there had been another loss, in St. Louis by just three points. Gore emerged from the medical room after an X-ray of his injured right ankle (negative) and sat down on a stool (short) in front of his dressing stall (empty) to discuss his mood (sad).

"It's tough, you know?" Gore said. "We played it tough. We didn't finish."[145]

Which is how the 49ers usually ended up their Sundays during Gore's first six seasons, from 2005 through 2010. Opposing teams would stack defenses against him, putting extra men in the box between the tackles. The 5-foot-9, 212-pound Gore would get his yards anyway. This earned him a pertinent nickname: "The Inconvenient Truth," inspired by former Vice President Al Gore (no relation) and his movie about climate change.

In that 2006 season full of ice packs, Gore was amazingly inconvenient. He set the franchise single-game rushing record with 212 yards on 24 carries against Seattle, as well as the 49er record for combined yardage—1,570 rushing, 535 receiving, 2,180 total.

The other vivid memory of Frank Gore is of the most earnest and sincere football player in the sport. After growing up in a one-bedroom Florida apartment with 11 other people, then being drafted in the third round out of Miami because scouts thought his college knee surgery had slowed him down, Gore took nothing for granted. He lived just down the street from the 49ers' practice facility in Santa Clara so that he could spend as many hours there as possible—or rehabilitate his injuries as intensely as possible.

This was why, when the 49ers at last hauled themselves out of their losing muck in 2011 under Jim Harbaugh, one of the biggest joys was seeing Gore's work ethic and tough yards being rewarded with winning seasons and playoff trips. Harbaugh might have been Gore's biggest fan. "What an unwavering competitor," Harbaugh once said. "If there's a football heaven, it's awaiting."[146]

Frank Gore rushed for a 49er record 212 yards against the Seattle Seahawks in a 2006 game.

COURTESY OF ROBERT B. STANTON/NFLPHOTOLIBRARY VIA GETTY IMAGES

Former 49ers players Steve Young, Dwight Hicks, and Joe Montana, along with Eddie DeBartolo and Carmen Policy, attend a public memorial service for former 49ers coach Bill Walsh on August 10, 2007.
COURTESY OF JUSTIN SULLIVAN/GETTY IMAGES

2007

Bill Walsh's Passing Marks the End of Something

S **BILL WALSH,** the most significant person in 49ers franchise history, died of blood and bone cancer on July 30, 2007. His memorial service at Stanford University's Memorial Church was attended by dozens of former players and marked by eulogies from Eddie DeBartolo, Joe Montana, and Dr. Harry Edwards, the social activist who had helped Walsh set up a 49ers' program for minority coaches that boosted many of their careers. As the service concluded, it felt like the end of something monumental.

Some people make a difference. Others literally are the difference. So it was with Walsh when it came to his impact in the region of the United States he loved the most.

Walsh was the Bay Area's best coach. In any sport. Ever. That's meant with no disrespect to Pop Warner, John Madden, Tony LaRussa, Bruce Bochy, Steve Kerr, or any of the other coaches whose accomplishments made their marks on the region. Walsh was a notch above them.

Upon induction into the Pro Football Hall of Fame in 1993, Walsh became the first native Californian to enter Canton as a coach. He represented not just himself but an entire culture and mindset. Bay Area citizens like to believe they are more open-minded, innovative, sophisticated, and creative than the rest of the nation. Walsh personified those qualities every Sunday afternoon. Dressed in his cream sweaters with headphones clamped down over his wispy white hair, scheming ways to beat his non-enlightened foes, he was the intellectual play caller.

Walsh transformed the 49ers into the Bay Area's premier sports entity. He also invented and introduced the West Coast Offense to a staid league that soon universally adopted it. That offense was based on being more clever and precise than opponents. Yet Walsh, a former amateur boxer, equally loved football's physical aspects. He was a much tougher guy than his popular image. In 1984, when Walsh had his best 49ers team, there was a certain adrenaline rush just entering Candlestick Park and seeing him pace the field before kickoff, knowing he had assembled a virtually unbeatable team with a virtually unstoppable game plan.

It was an almost perfect Bay Area sports picture. When Walsh passed away, he took that picture with him. There won't be another like him.

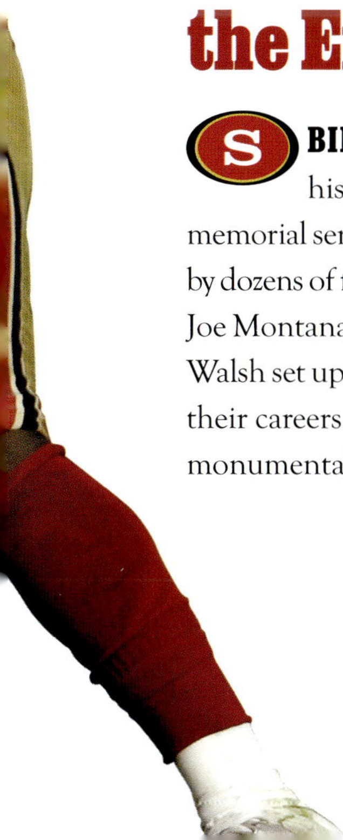

2007

Bryant Young Retires

BRYANT YOUNG felt his right knee come apart one day in November 2005. He was playing defensive end for the 49ers at the time. So, this was not a good thing. And with his team slogging its way to a third consecutive miserable losing record, not many people figured they would see Young on a football field again that season.

He was back the next month. Young, following his surgery for a torn medial collateral ligament, did some rapid rehab and suited up for a December road game that ended in yet another agonizing loss. In his 12th NFL season and as the only Niner player left from the Super Bowl XXIX team, Young was entitled to cut himself some slack and miss that game. Not a possibility. If you're a pro and you can play, you play. He played.

"It's almost like a character check," Young said. "It really tests your integrity. I just wanted to make sure I was doing what was right."[147]

There might be no 49er player, current or former, who was more respected than Bryant Young in his playing days. When he announced his retirement in 2007, there was an unmistakable void in the roster. Eight times, the 49er players voted him the winner of the Len Eshmont Award for "inspirational and courageous" play.

On the field, at 6-foot-3 and 300 pounds, Young controlled the line of scrimmage as few men could. If his assignment was to draw a double team block to free up other pass rushers, he was fine with that. He spent all 14 years of his career with the 49ers and racked up 89.5 sacks, the most in franchise history. In 1998 during a Monday night game, he suffered a broken tibia and fibula. He had a titanium rod inserted to mend the leg back together, then returned in the 1999 season to accumulate 11 sacks and be named the NFL's Comeback Player of the Year.

When he was elected to the Pro Football Hall of Fame in 2022, tributes abounded. Former 49er quarterback Jeff Garcia may have uttered the finest compliment when he simply said: "Everybody should have the opportunity to have a teammate like that."[148]

Defensive tackle Bryant Young had a Hall of Fame career with the 49ers, with 89.5 sacks and three safeties.

COURTESY OF NHAT V. MEYER/MEDIANEWS GROUP/BAY AREA NEWS VIA GETTY IMAGES

Harbaugh Changes the Culture to Khaki

JED YORK was only 27 years old in 2009 when his parents, Denise and John York, handed him the keys to the CEO office at 49er headquarters. After firing head coach Mike Singletary near the end of the 2010 season, York set his sights on Jim Harbaugh down the road at Stanford. Harbaugh had just won the Orange Bowl after a 12–1 season, making him a trendy commodity on the coaching market. York offered Harbaugh a five-year deal for $25 million, a staggering amount at that time. There were skeptics. Harbaugh had never coached an NFL game. His personality was a little loopy.

"I hope to be very underestimated," Harbaugh said at his introductory press conference.[149]

It would be safe to say that the underestimators were overwrong. Harbaugh inherited a 49er team that had gone nine seasons without a playoff appearance. Between his motivational tactics and his X's and O's, he executed a turnaround of Golden Gate Bridge–sized proportions. The 49ers won nine of their first 10 games, finished atop the NFC West, and compiled a 13–3 record. Niner alum Ronnie Lott called it "one of the greatest coaching jobs in the history of coaching."[150]

How did Harbaugh do it? Much media attention went to his quirky individuality and peculiar habits. Harbaugh wore generic khaki pants every day so he wouldn't have to waste a minute making wardrobe choices. He used strange analogies. He led players in a corny call-and-response cheer that his father had invented to convince the Harbaugh kids to appreciate their opportunities: "Who's got it better than us?" The proper response, as every 49er fan came to memorize, was: "Noooooooobody."

Harbaugh coached with fire and didn't care who in the NFL he offended. His feud with Seattle coach Pete Carroll was long running. After a victory in Detroit, Harbaugh backslapped Lions coach Jim Schwartz a smidgen too forcefully and Schwartz initiated a shoving match.

These self-inflicted sideshows obscured Harbaugh's impressive strategic moves. He retooled the offense to better suit quarterback Alex Smith's skill set. He lined up tight end Delanie Walker in 15 different spots on the scrimmage line or in the backfield or split out. He moved offensive linemen into different slots if he spotted a weak link on an opposing defensive line. He installed blocking schemes to take advantage of Frank Gore's seam-finding, slide-and-sprint running style.

The only thing Harbaugh couldn't do during his four 49er seasons was win a Super Bowl. But he came damn close.

Head coach Jim Harbaugh did a phenomenal job in his first season with the 49ers in 2011 and was named Coach of the Year.

COURTESY OF PETER G. AIKEN/GETTY IMAGES

January 14, 2012

Vernon Davis and Alex Smith Bring Back Playoff Magic

WHEN THE 49ers ended their lengthy postseason drought with a miracle 2011 turnaround, they gave the NFL a playoff game for the ages at Candlestick Park.

By the closing seconds of their 36–32 victory over the New Orleans Saints—in which the lead changed hands four times during the final five minutes—Niners offensive tackle Joe Staley felt as if he had aged 20 years.

"It was surreal," said Staley. "It was crazy. It was amazing. Everybody talks about what it will be like. And you can anticipate it, but the overall atmosphere . . . I'm exhausted. I'm physically drained."[151]

Fans felt the same way. The contest lasted 3 hours and 42 minutes.

"This," said coach Jim Harbaugh, "was an all-day sucker."[152]

The game's final few whipsaw minutes, by themselves, constituted a heroic novel. The heavily favored Saints scored a touchdown with 4:02 left to take a 24–23 lead. A thrilling 28-yard TD run by Alex Smith pushed the 49ers back ahead. But the Saints needed only 34 seconds for quarterback Drew Brees to regain the lead, 32–29.

Thus, with 14 seconds remaining, the 49ers needed a field goal to tie and send the game into overtime. They instead went for broke. More specifically, they went for tight end Vernon Davis, who had already made six important catches at key moments throughout the afternoon.

On third down at the 14-yard line, Harbaugh rolled the dice for "Vernon Post," a play installed days earlier just for such a situation. Davis dug downfield over the middle into the end zone, then turned around and used his body to box out a defender. Smith, who since 2005 had been criticized for his inaccurate throws at crunch time, this time spun the ball perfectly to Davis. With a Saints defensive back clawing at Davis's shoulders, he came down with the winning points. Davis then ran, weeping, toward the sidelines. The play, four days after the 30th anniversary of "The Catch," was dubbed "The Grab" by the man who made it.

"This is huge for us," said Davis. "It's history, legendary, anything you can describe."[153]

It was also redemption. Davis had turned his career around after coach Mike Singletary had benched him in 2008, and had made himself into one of the game's best tight ends. Not even a bitter 20–17 overtime loss to the New York Giants in the NFC Championship Game could fully erase the glow of Davis's triumphant moment. Anticipation swelled for the 2012 season.

Vernon Davis makes a key catch during the NFC divisional playoff game against the New Orleans Saints. His last-minute game-winner was dubbed "The Catch III" or "The Grab."

COURTESY OF JOSE CARLOS FAJARDO/MEDIANEWS GROUP/BAY AREA NEWS VIA GETTY IMAGES

Alex Smith's Concussion Is Colin Kaepernick's Big Break

COLIN KAEPERNICK had about 10 seconds to find his helmet, then about 90 seconds to warm up his arm. The second-year quarterback from the University of Nevada was Alex Smith's backup in 2012 when Smith suffered a concussion in the second quarter of a 24–24 tie with the St. Louis Rams in Week 10.

Kaepernick didn't set off fireworks in his first extensive NFL action. He didn't stink up the joint, either. His stat line read 11-for-17 for 117 yards, plus eight scrambles for 66 yards and a touchdown.

How could he have known what was ahead? How could anyone? Kaepernick did not expect to start the following week, let alone the rest of the season, let alone in the Super Bowl three months later. But that's where fate propelled him after the following two Sundays—a 32–7 rout of the Chicago Bears and an impressive 31–21 victory over the Saints. Kaepernick demonstrated that he was something unique and extraordinary, something the NFL wasn't sure how to process.

It had nothing to do with his tattoos, which also were unique and extraordinary. Kaepernick was a 6-foot-4, 235-pound unicorn. He had a bazooka arm combined with long legs that, in the open field, let him accelerate like no other NFL quarterback. In college, Kaepernick had adeptly operated a read-option offense, so the 49er coaches inserted some read-option concepts into the game plans. He gave the 49ers, who at that point were largely a Frank-Gore-running-game operation, an extra dimension.

It was obvious that Kaepernick was a stronger thrower with faster feet than Smith. But Jim Harbaugh couldn't say this when he was asked why Smith, who was leading the league in completion percentage with a passer rating of 104.1, had lost his starting job simply by getting hurt. So, Harbaugh maintained that in his mind, Kaepernick and Smith were co-starters. "Both have earned it," Harbaugh explained, but "Colin has the hot hand. We'll go with Colin."[154]

The hot hand never cooled. Smith bit his tongue and demonstrated his professionalism by standing on the sideline and trying to look supportive. Kaepernick went 7–3 as a starter and produced 2,229 yards of total offense and 15 touchdowns while averaging 8.3 yards per pass attempt and 6.6 yards per carry. His controversial social protests were in the future. In 2012, the 49ers' new offensive unicorn was a marvel to behold.

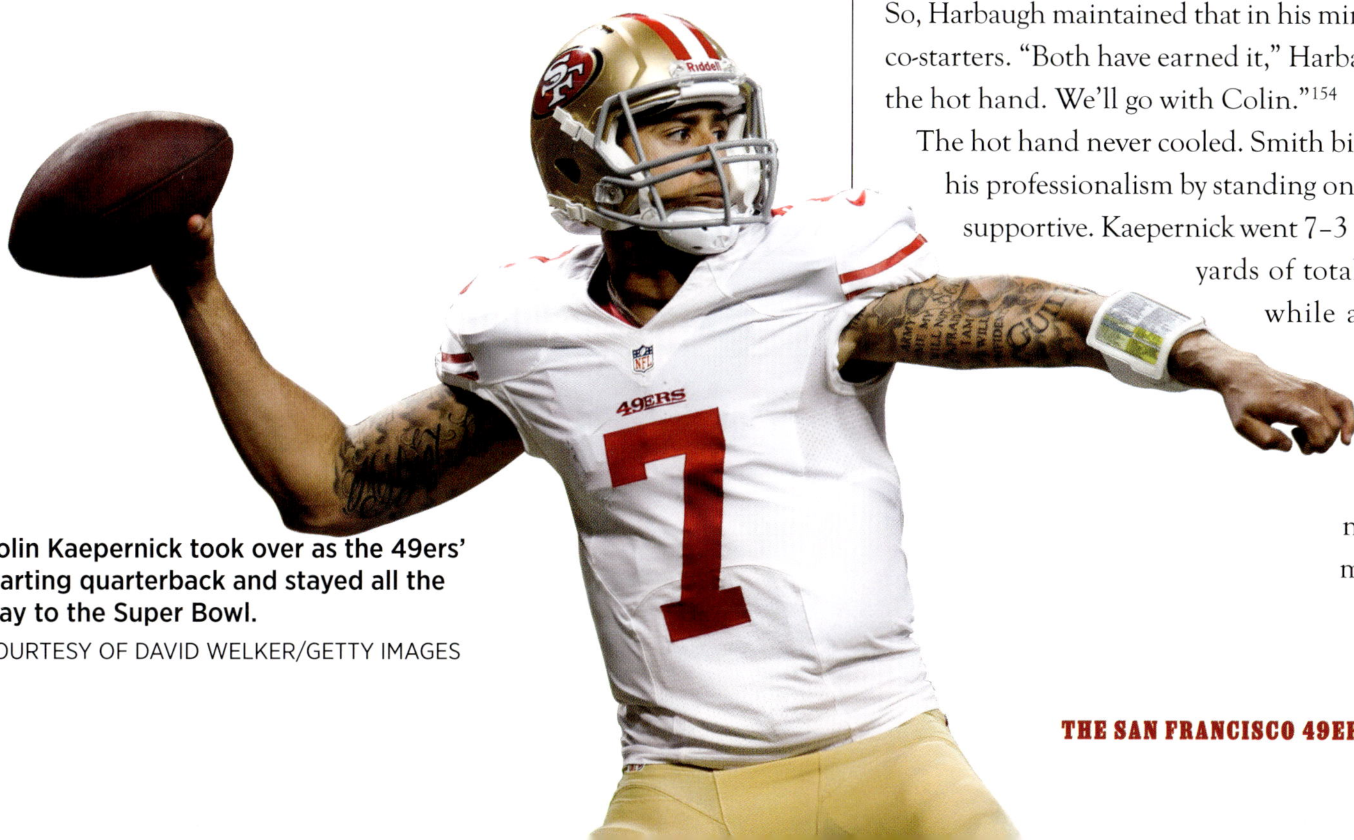

Colin Kaepernick took over as the 49ers' starting quarterback and stayed all the way to the Super Bowl.

COURTESY OF DAVID WELKER/GETTY IMAGES

The Green Bay Packers couldn't keep up with Colin Kaepernick in the NFC Divisional Game in 2013. The quarterback set a record with 181 rushing yards and two touchdowns.

COURTESY OF HARRY HOW/GETTY IMAGES

"Did He Just Do That?" Kaepernick's Run to the Super Bowl

THE QUESTION before the 2012 playoffs began was whether the inexperienced Colin Kaepernick could handle the postseason pressure and adversity. The answer was a big fat yes. Also, a big *fast* yes.

The 49ers' unexpected run to the Super Bowl was a blur of Kaepernick sprints that left opposing tacklers in his wake. Each of their two victories to reach New Orleans was a tour de force by the Niners' shooting-star quarterback, with valued help from his supporting cast.

First up was a 45–31 victory over Green Bay at Candlestick Park. Kaepernick rushed for 181 yards, more yardage than any NFL quarterback had generated on foot in any game ever. In his first postseason start—and just his eighth NFL start period—Kaepernick scored touchdowns on runs of 20 and 56 yards. Observers on both sidelines were left slack jawed.

"I'm standing there saying, 'Wow, did he just do that?'" said 49ers linebacker Patrick Willis.[155]

"We didn't really have a whole lot of answers for him," said Green Bay quarterback Aaron Rodgers.[156]

Kaepernick threw for 263 yards and two touchdowns. He also forced Green Bay defenders to concentrate on his read-option edge runs, creating space for Frank Gore in the middle and 49er receivers everywhere. Green Bay's defenders had to account for Kaepernick's legs before worrying about his arm—not to mention the chip on his shoulder.

"A lot of people doubted my ability to lead this team," Kaepernick said. "People say I'm just a running quarterback that is kind of raw. I think there is a huge difference between being a running quarterback and a quarterback that can run. I see that as something a little disrespectful."[157]

He took that same attitude to Atlanta the following week. The Falcons jumped out to a 17–0 lead, but that merely set the stage for the biggest comeback victory in NFC Championship Game history. The Niners outscored the Falcons 28–7 over the game's final 38 minutes to win 28–24.

The Falcons' focus on Kaepernick's run threat allowed Gore to produce 90 rushing yards and two touchdowns, including the game winner, when he was barely touched. The fired-up San Francisco defense shut out Atlanta in the second half. The most critical stop was on fourth down at the 10-yard line with 1:13 remaining. During a timeout just before the play, Kaepernick stepped onto the turf and yelled, "This is for the Super Bowl! I've got confidence in you!"[158]

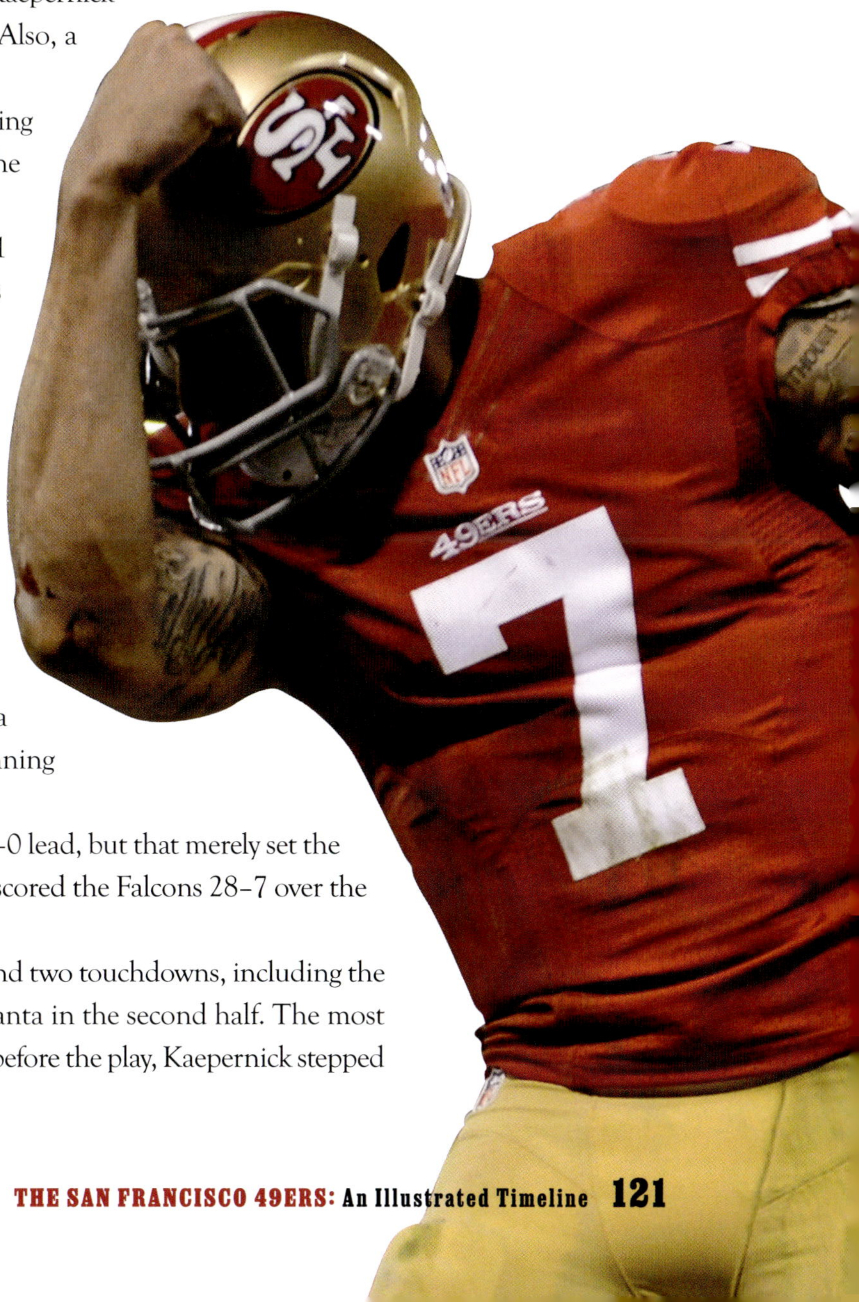

The bicep kiss was Colin Kaepernick's signature celebration.

COURTESY OF HARRY HOW/ GETTY IMAGES

Niners running back Frank Gore breaks a tackle attempted by Baltimore Ravens cornerback Corey Graham on his way to a touchdown in Super Bowl XLVII.

COURTESY OF MIKE EHRMANN/GETTY IMAGES

Super Bowl XLVII: Blacked Out and Edged Out

SUPER BOWL XLVII was the Sibling Bowl, matching up 49ers coach Jim Harbaugh against his brother, John Harbaugh, head coach of the Baltimore Ravens. It was a Super Bowl first. The brothers met pregame expectations at their New Orleans press sessions by quoting a Harbaugh family bromide.

"We're attacking this day with an enthusiasm unknown to mankind," said 49ers coach Jim.[159]

"We're topping that," countered Ravens coach John.[160]

Baltimore blitzed its way to a 28–6 lead in the third quarter with sharp execution by quarterback Joe Flacco along with Jacoby Jones's 108-yard kick return. Then the power and lights went out at the Superdome.

The 34-minute delay seemed to sap Baltimore's momentum. The 49ers stormed back, sparked by solid Colin Kaepernick playmaking.

The Niners were just five points behind, 34–29, and poised to win with 2:39 remaining in the game. But their offense blew a golden chance with a strange set of play calls.

On first down at the Baltimore 7-yard line, did the 49ers pound the ball in with Gore? No. Did they have Kaepernick run the read-option? They did not. Offensive coordinator Greg Roman, brilliantly creative all season, picked a bad series to have a bad series. On first down, backup running back LaMichael James gained two yards. On second down, Kaepernick couldn't find an open man. On third down, a play-action pass went incomplete, all receivers covered. On fourth down, Kaepernick lofted the ball to Michael Crabtree on a fade pattern. He and the Ravens' Jimmy Smith placed hands on each other but there was no penalty call.

The fourth-down pass is just out of Michael Crabtree's reach in the final moments of Super Bowl XLVII.

COURTESY OF EZRA SHAW/GETTY IMAGES

Baltimore purposely took a safety, and the game was over. Baltimore players said they were surprised Gore hadn't touched the ball on the last 49er series. When reporters asked Jim Harbaugh why that had been the case, he said: "We had other plays called."[161]

Baltimore was a worthy champion. But in the Bay Area, the encounter will always be remembered as a game the 49ers lost, not a game the Ravens won. "I respect them," Frank Gore said. "But we're the better team."[162]

NaVorro Bowman returns an interception 89 yards for a touchdown, electrifying the Candlestick Park crowd in the 49ers' last game in the storied stadium.

COURTESY OF MICHAEL ZAGARIS/ SAN FRANCISCO 49ERS/GETTY IMAGES

December 23, 2013

Bowman's "Pick at the Stick" on Goodbye Night

WITH A new stadium in Santa Clara on the horizon, the 49ers put on their party hats and gave dank old Candlestick Park a farewell salute on December 23, 2013. It would turn out to be a spectacular exclamation point.

After falling behind 10–3 at halftime, the Niners scored 31 points in the final two quarters against the Atlanta Falcons and finished off the last scheduled NFL game inside San Francisco's city limits with a 34–24 victory.

Before the opening kickoff, 49ers owner Jed York—who had spearheaded the effort to build the new Levi's Stadium that was coming in 2014—stood on the sideline and soaked in the scene. He did not feel nostalgic, York said. "It just feels . . . weird," he said. "You know?"[163]

The evening would become weirder still. In a preposterous yet fitting finish for the 53-year-old concrete funhouse, Candlestick's concluding touchdown was scored not by a wide receiver or running back, but by 49ers linebacker NaVorro Bowman.

Minutes earlier, Bowman had positioned himself to become the game's goat. He lost the handle on an onside kick return, and with 2:09 remaining Atlanta recovered the ball. The Falcons' offense, trailing by just three points, moved within 10 yards of the end zone. That's when Bowman gained unlikely redemption. He closed in on a bobbled Falcons pass reception, snatched the ball out of the air, and returned it 89 yards for a dramatic, game-clinching touchdown. As he tumbled into the end zone, the 69,732 throats in attendance began chanting: "CANDLE-STICK, CANDLE-STICK, CANDLE-STICK."

"That's the best thing I've ever seen happen in a football game," said Niners coach Jim Harbaugh, caught up in the moment.[164]

Bowman's play would come to be known as "The Pick at the Stick." After the clock expired, a stage was rolled out for speeches. Steve Young and Jerry Rice waved to the crowd. York presented the game ball to his uncle, former 49ers owner Eddie DeBartolo Jr.

Music played. Lights dimmed. Fireworks exploded in a large circle outside the stadium. Most everyone went home happy—and ridiculously slowly, as was traditional with Candlestick's poor ingress and egress. It might have been the worst stadium in the NFL. But it was a dump with a glorious history.

Another Playoff Run Falls a CenturyLink Short

THERE WAS still some mystery about whether the 49ers' run to the Super Bowl in 2012 had been a one-off mirage. Colin Kaepernick and the team had a lot more to prove in 2013.

And they did. Adding veteran receiver Anquan Boldin gave Kaepernick another toy for his toybox. With the Pro Bowl ascent of linebackers NaVorro Bowman and Patrick Willis, the Niners' defense helped boost the team's record to 12–4. The problem: Seattle finished 13–3 and won the NFC West. This meant the playoffs would be a road gantlet—with a frozen entrance ramp.

The 49ers kicked off the postseason at Green Bay's Lambeau Field in 5-degree weather with a minus-10 wind chill—and dropping. The Packers were consensus frostbite favorites. But the Niners earned their coldest playoff victory in history, 23–20, with a Phil Dawson field goal on the game's last play. Kaepernick used up the final 5:06 on the scoreboard to set it up, milking the cold clock to perfection.

The following Sunday in Charlotte, the temperature was 44 degrees warmer. The 49ers took care of business, beating the Carolina Panthers 23–10. After Kaepernick ran for a third-quarter touchdown, he went beyond his usual biceps-kiss "Kaepernicking." He also mocked the "ripping open the Superman suit" gesture of Carolina quarterback Cam Newton, who was picked first overall in the same 2011 draft where Kaepernick was the 36th man selected.

The next 49er task was to win a third road playoff game in three weeks. Not even Superman could do that. Playing the NFC title game at Seattle's unruly CenturyLink Field compounded the challenge. In a wicked and brutal 23–17 defeat, the Niners lost Bowman to a torn ACL and MCL in his left knee. Offensive lineman Mike Iupati broke his ankle. And yet, San Francisco led 17–10 before Kaepernick's miserable fourth quarter when he fumbled and threw an interception. His last-gasp end-zone throw to Michael Crabtree was batted upward by Seattle's Richard Sherman and snatched by teammate Malcolm Smith.

Jim Harbaugh called the game "a 15-round fight" that the 49ers had "lost in the final round."[165] He could have been describing the entire playoff journey.

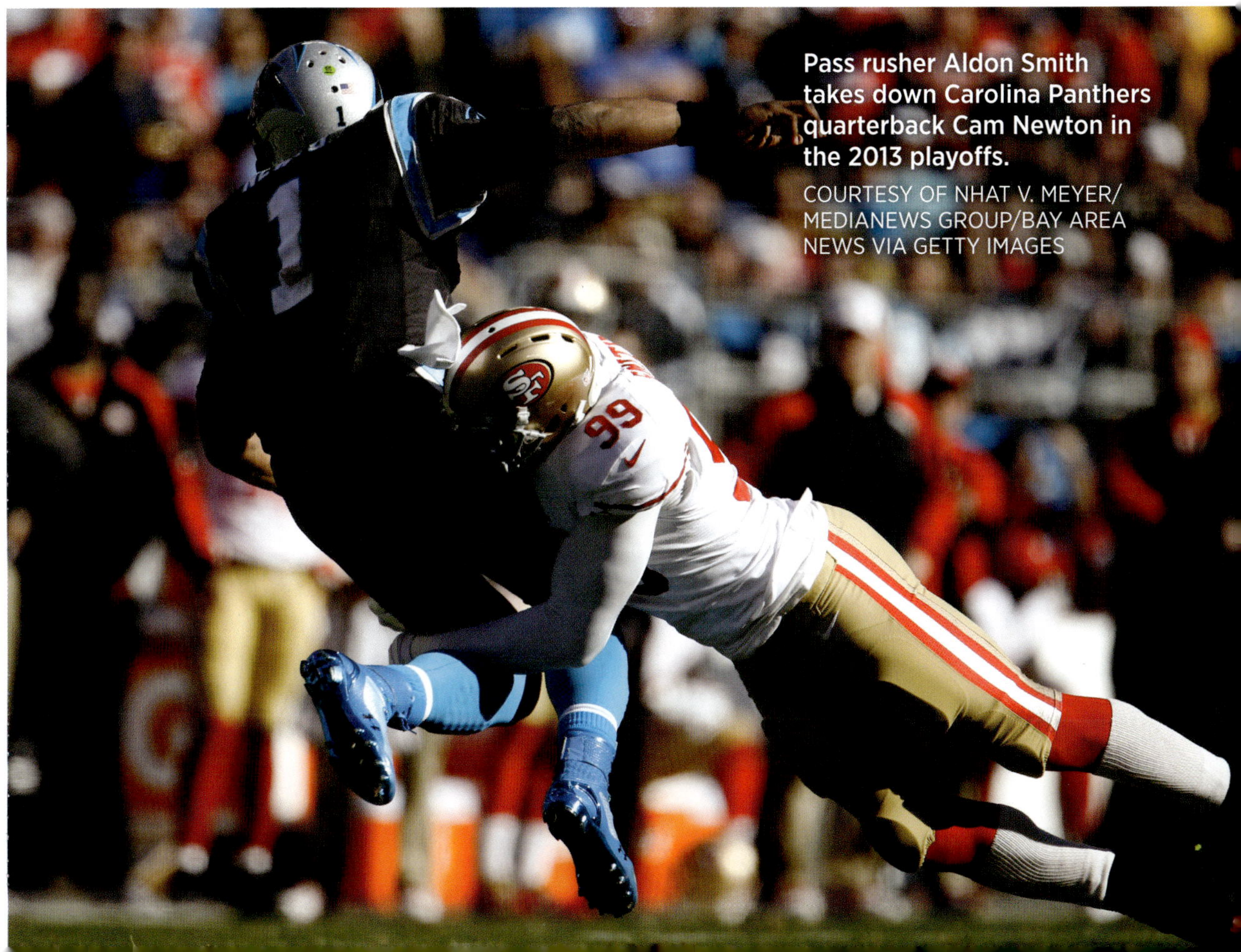

Pass rusher Aldon Smith takes down Carolina Panthers quarterback Cam Newton in the 2013 playoffs.

COURTESY OF NHAT V. MEYER/ MEDIANEWS GROUP/BAY AREA NEWS VIA GETTY IMAGES

The 49ers' new home, Levi's Stadium, opened in 2014, but in Santa Clara rather than in San Francisco.
COURTESY OF EZRA SHAW/GETTY IMAGES

Levi's Stadium: New Digs in Santa Clara

THE FIRST regular season game at the 49ers' new Levi's Stadium in Santa Clara was a deflated balloon in terms of football. History records that on September 14, 2014, with 70,799 guests yelling enthusiastically, the 49ers perpetrated an unsightly collapse as the Chicago Bears came back from a 17–0 deficit to win 28–20.

"It was very disappointing," said Niners linebacker Ahmad Brooks. "When it's a new stadium and when the 49ers organization has so much history behind them."[166]

The defeat did not diminish the evening's most amazing fact: San Francisco's professional football team, after endless years of trying to get a modern stadium built, had completed its $1.3 billion mission. Granted, the structure was not in San Francisco. But its location meshed perfectly with the "so much history" cited by Brooks. Levi's Stadium was constructed just five miles north of the Santa Clara University campus where, eight decades earlier, team founder Tony Morabito had lit the spark that grew into the 49ers franchise. You might say the team had come full circle.

Getting there wasn't easy. A plan for a new stadium on the old Candlestick site, with a shopping mall attached, had fallen through. The 49ers then rejected San Francisco's proposal for a Hunter's Point site that was a former naval shipyard contaminated with hazardous waste. Instead, the Yorks cast their gaze 44 miles south to a parking lot outside the Great America amusement park. The site also conveniently adjoined the 49ers' training headquarters and executive offices, where they'd done business since 1988.

As the first NFL-specific venue built in California, Levi's Stadium included a 49ers museum celebrating the team's history. The stadium had concourses that were 43 feet wider than Candlestick's, plus 250 more toilets. Premium seating included a suite tower and rooftop eco-garden. There were gripes that the team had "abandoned" San Francisco, even though the team had trained and practiced in Santa Clara 355 days a year for the previous 30 years. Business-wise, the move made sense. Given the growth of Silicon Valley, far more Fortune 500 companies (and potential sponsors) were based in Santa Clara County than in San Francisco. San Jose, the Bay Area's largest city, also bordered Santa Clara.

The 49ers Museum features several statues of players and figures from the team's history, including Joe Montana and Bill Walsh.

COURTESY OF MARK PURDY

At the ribbon-cutting ceremony, Levi's chief executive Chip Bergh called the 49ers' new home "the most amazing stadium on the face of the planet."[167] But stadiums are only made amazing if amazing stuff happens inside them. The 49ers were responsible for taking care of that. In time, they would.

Changes and Turmoil Wreck a Good Thing

AS JIM Harbaugh entered his fourth season with the 49ers, tension was apparent. He and general manager Trent Baalke did not see eye to eye on personnel moves. Jed York was growing weary of Harbaugh's high-maintenance eccentricities. There were internal disputes about how to deal with the 10 times that players were arrested between 2012 and 2014 on charges ranging from domestic violence to driving under the influence. A happy time, it wasn't.

After starting the 2014 season with a 4–4 record, the Niners won three straight to set up a Thanksgiving Day showdown with Seattle at Levi's Stadium—and laid a huge egg. After the desultory 19–3 loss, much to Harbaugh's displeasure, York used his Twitter account for an apology to fans ("This performance wasn't acceptable. I apologize for that."[168]). The 49ers lost their next four games. Rumors gurgled about the front office trading Harbaugh, or that he would become head coach at the University of Michigan. The Michigan rumors came true.

In a strange final Sunday of the season, the 49ers beat Arizona as a press release circulated that Harbaugh and the team had "mutually agreed to part ways." Harbaugh used his postgame news session to say he'd been "proud" to work for the Yorks.

The surprising and ultimately dreadful choice to replace Harbaugh was assistant coach Jim Tomsula, who was in over his head and dismissed after a single 5–11 season. By then, the 49ers' talent pool had been diluted by the departures of free agent Frank Gore to Indianapolis and linebacker Patrick Willis to retirement at age 30.

Willis played only eight NFL seasons. He made them memorable ones with six Pro Bowl selections and a reputation as a whirling-ball-of-knives tackler. His speedy feet could take him from sideline to sideline. His hits were vicious and true. Willis openly proclaimed that his goal was to reach the Pro Football Hall of Fame. With his 2024 induction, he did.

After Tomsula's firing, York told reporters, "You have to learn from failure—we need to make sure we get the next one right."[169] Then York stumbled again by hiring Chip Kelly, who went 2–14 and blew 10 first-half leads, saddled with the weak roster assembled by Baalke. Both of them were fired at season's end. Baalke admitted it was "the right thing to do" because "sometimes, you need to reset the culture."[170]

Fierce 49ers linebacker Patrick Willis terrorized opponents during his Hall of Fame career.
COURTESY OF JED JACOBSOHN/GETTY IMAGES

Kaepernick Brings the NFL to His Knees

THE PHRASE "taking a knee" in the NFL once had an entirely different meaning. Colin Kaepernick changed the definition. In doing so, he both inspired and enraged an entire sport and nation.

During the 2016 preseason, Kaepernick purposely stayed seated on the bench during the singing of the national anthem to protest recent police killings of Black citizens. After a discussion with former NFL player and military veteran Nate Boyer, Kaepernick altered the protest and knelt on one knee during the song, feeling it was more respectful.

Millions disagreed. From coast to coast, Kaepernick was condemned for being unpatriotic or worse. Millions of others supported him. Athletes copied his protest before games at high schools and colleges, as did several NFL players. The league released a statement saying players were "encouraged but not required" to stand during the anthem.[171] Politicians of all persuasions weighed in with their own opinionated speechifying. The dichotomy was startling. Videos of angry fans burning Kaepernick's No. 7 jersey dominated social media. Yet the same No. 7 jersey was the top seller at NFL.com. In a league where 68 percent of the workforce was Black, teammates and opponents lent words of support. Kaepernick kept kneeling. And speaking up.

"At the end of the day, I'm going to continue to fight for what I believe," he said.[172]

Meanwhile, he was also trying to play football. Kaepernick was not 100 percent back from shoulder surgery, so 49ers head coach Chip Kelly used Blaine Gabbert for the first five games of the season. Kaepernick made his first start in October at Buffalo. Vendors outside the stadium sold bootleg T-shirts that featured his likeness in the crosshairs of a gun sight. Whenever he was tackled in the 45–16 loss, fans chanted, "U-S-A, U-S-A."

Colin Kaepernick, center, sparked a national controversy by kneeling during the national anthem as a protest. Teammates Eli Harold (left) and Eric Reid (right) kneel with him.

COURTESY OF MICHAEL ZAGARIS/SAN FRANCISCO 49ERS/GETTY IMAGES

Every subsequent Sunday was a combination sociology pageant and athletic contest. Kaepernick was inconsistent and ineffective, then showed up for postgame media sessions wearing a Fidel Castro T-shirt or socks that portrayed policemen as pigs. Kelly claimed that Kaepernick was "zero distraction." But the weekly news cameras in the locker room surely contributed to the Niners' miserable 2–14 record.

At season's end, Kaepernick asked for his release before the 49ers could cut him. No other NFL team has since signed him. In 2017, feeling the league had blackballed him, Kaepernick sued the league and reached a settlement. There's no doubt Kaepernick's career was cut short by his activist choices. His brief chapter in 49er history stands out for more than just kneeling down. But that image will always be his yearbook picture.

Reaching to the heavens, 49ers running back Christian McCaffrey catches a touchdown pass against the Los Angeles Rams in 2022.
COURTESY OF RONALD MARTINEZ/GETTY IMAGES

CHAPTER 6 THE QUEST FOR SIX 2017–

TWENTY YEARS AFTER the 49ers' last Super Bowl win, Jed York was impatient. In 2014, the owner explained why he and coach Jim Harbaugh had parted ways, despite winning an NFC title and two division titles.

"It's up to us to make sure we compete for and win Super Bowls," York said. "That's our only goal. We don't raise division championship banners. We don't raise NFC Championship banners. We raise Super Bowl banners."[173]

So far, not yet under York. On the heels of his brash statement, the 49ers rolled out a promotional campaign called "Quest for Six." It was meant to be aspirational, said marketing director Ali Towle, because "a quest is by its very nature challenging."[174]

As the 49ers would learn. And learn. And learn. During the ensuing 10 years, there was much questing. But still no championship. Under head coach Kyle Shanahan, the 49ers have provided captivating football with two glorious Super Bowl trips . . . and two galling Super Bowl losses. The questing continues. > > >

Shanahan and Lynch's Learning Curve Straightens

AFTER THE Jim Tomsula and Chip Kelly oil spills, the 49ers' cleanup crew turned out to be Kyle Shanahan and John Lynch. They were hired in January 2017. This time, Jed York got it right.

Kyle Shanahan

COURTESY OF MICHAEL ZAGARIS/SAN FRANCISCO 49ERS/GETTY IMAGES

Shanahan, 37, was an experienced and successful offensive coordinator for the Atlanta Falcons who had just played in the Super Bowl—where he was criticized for his play calling after the Falcons blew a lead and lost the game. But his reputation for creativity and smarts preceded him. Kyle was also the son of Mike Shanahan, who had coached two Super Bowl champions in Denver while giving Kyle an education in how to grow thick skin.

Lynch, 46, was hired upon Shanahan's recommendation and was the far riskier choice. After an All-Pro playing career as a safety, Lynch had spent eight seasons as a television analyst. He possessed lots of NFL knowledge. He possessed zero experience as an executive.

The two did know the Bay Area, though. Lynch had played football and baseball at Stanford. Shanahan had attended school in Saratoga during his dad's two seasons as the 49ers' offensive coordinator.

"I remember spending all my summers up in Rocklin at 49er training camp as a ball boy," Kyle said at his introductory press conference. "I had a little rollout bed in my dad's room."[175]

Now, Kyle was in charge of the big-boy furniture. And Lynch was the furniture delivery man. Their learning curve was steep and had some glitches. Which is a nice way of saying that in their initial 49er draft, with two first-round picks at their disposal, Lynch and Shanahan essentially whiffed. They selected defensive lineman Solomon Thomas of Stanford and linebacker Reuben Foster of Alabama. Both were underwhelming and non-impactful. Thomas, in four 49er seasons, accumulated just six sacks before he left San Francisco as a free agent. Foster was frequently injured and always in trouble. After multiple arrests for domestic violence and possession of an illegal weapon, he was released.

Fortunately, Shanahan and Lynch did not take long to straighten out their learning curve. They drafted a certain tight end in the 2017 draft's fifth round. And, after muddling through the first months of the 2017 season with a grab-bag of thrift-store quarterbacks, they traded for a better looking one. The two men would immediately change the 49ers' trajectory—upward.

John Lynch

COURTESY OF STACY REVERE/GETTY IMAGES

Jed York

COURTESY OF STEPH CHAMBERS/GETTY IMAGES

Owner Jed York hired general manager John Lynch and head coach Kyle Shanahan, with the goal of leading the 49ers to a sixth Lombardi Trophy.

The 49ers traded for quarterback Jimmy Garoppolo in 2017, and he won his first five starts.

COURTESY OF ZACH BOLINGER/ICON SPORTSWIRE VIA GETTY IMAGES

2017

Jimmy G and the Birth of Handsome Hope

KYLE SHANAHAN took two months to decide that Brian Hoyer was not his quarterback of the future. Before the 2017 season, the 49ers had signed free agent Hoyer after the team's parting of ways with Colin Kaepernick. Hoyer had been with six different NFL organizations. He was waived by the Niners after starting six games.

The next contestant for the job was C. J. Beathard, the rookie out of Iowa. Pick another category, please. By the end of October, the overmatched Beathard and the Niners were 0–8. Shanahan and general manager John Lynch had to do something. Lynch picked up the phone. He closed a deal with the New England Patriots for Jimmy Garoppolo, who was Tom Brady's backup, for a second-round pick.

Garoppolo had played college ball at lower-tier Eastern Illinois, so he was not well known, even after subbing in for Brady twice and winning both games. But one part of his reputation did precede him: His chiseled good looks. When tight end George Kittle heard about the trade with New England, Kittle's first reaction was: "Holy Cow, Jimmy Garoppolo, that chin, finally making its way to the West Coast."[176]

Garoppolo's throwing arm was the more important asset. After taking a few weeks to learn the 49ers system, he made his first start at Chicago on December 3. After he beat the Bears 15–14, love blossomed with the Niners' fan base. That romance grew exponentially as Garoppolo—now known as "Jimmy G" —reeled off five straight victories to finish the season, averaging 308.4 passing yards per start, with seven touchdowns against five interceptions.

Garoppolo became a free agent after the final game, but the 49ers did not want to lose him. They signed him to a five-year contract worth $137.5 million. At the time, it was the largest NFL contract in history and a wacky amount of money for a still largely unproven player. But how can you put a price on hope? That's what Garoppolo represented. In his case, it was handsome hope. For the first time in four years, fans were looking forward to the next season.

George Kittle Breaks Out and Breaks the Mold

IF GEORGE Kittle did not exist, the NFL would have to invent him. After entering the league in 2017 as a fifth-round pick following a quiet college career at the University of Iowa, Kittle did nothing but make noise. In a good way. His outward-bound and anything-goes personality as the self-proclaimed "People's Tight End," combined with his embrace of physical play and first-down catches, could serve as an instruction manual for how to connect with professional football consumers.

As a rookie, Kittle started seven games, caught 48 passes for 515 yards and two touchdowns. Not bad. But nothing special.

That special stuff began a year later in his breakout season. Which happened despite the circumstances. In Week 3, Jimmy Garoppolo was tackled on a scramble and tore his left knee's ACL. He was done for the year. Presumptive running back starter Jerick McKinnon had already torn an ACL in training camp. The 49ers' offensive options dwindled. Kittle filled the breach. Backup quarterbacks C. J. Beathard and Nick Mullens found him an easy target.

Week after week as the 49ers slogged through a 4–12 season, Kittle's catches—and his runs after catches—were often the main reason to watch their games. In Week 14 against the Denver Broncos, he gained 210 yards on just seven catches, one for an 85-yard touchdown. That pushed Kittle over 1,000 yards for the season, a franchise first for tight end.

"When the ball is in the air, the play is just starting for George," said Shanahan. "He runs angry and is confident he's going to score."[177]

On the season's final day, Travis Kelce of the Kansas City Chiefs set an NFL single-season receiving yards record for a tight end with 1,336 yards. Kittle broke that record an hour later and finished with 1,377.

In 2019, Kittle would produce his signature moment in a high-scoring game against the New Orleans Saints, with both teams vying for the No. 1 playoff seed. On a fourth-down play from the Niners' own 33-yard line, down by a point with just 39 seconds left, Kittle took a short pass from Garoppolo and carried three defenders on his back—one grabbing his face mask—and refused to go down for 39 yards. It set up the game-winning field goal.

Shortly thereafter, Kittle successfully lobbied for a "National Tight Ends Day," which the NFL now celebrates on the fourth Sunday of every October. The people approve.

George Kittle, known as "The People's Tight End," makes his "zero fear" hand gesture after a touchdown.

COURTESY OF THEARON W. HENDERSON/ GETTY IMAGES

Dre Greenlaw (right) stops Seahawks tight end Jacob Hollister short of the goal line on fourth down with an assist from Fred Warner.

COURTESY OF MICHAEL ZAGARIS/SAN FRANCISCO 49ERS/GETTY IMAGES

2019

A Stop Sign at the 1-Yard Line

NOW AND then in the NFL, all the pieces fall into place and everyone is happy. Players. Coaches. Fans. Stadium beer vendors. All happy. Even if they're not exactly sure how it all happened. That was 2019 for the 49ers. In the franchise's greatest one-year turnaround, they improved from a 4–12 record to 13–3 and earned an NFC West title, two playoff victories, and a Super Bowl trip.

First lesson learned: beginning the season with an eight-game winning streak is happily helpful. So is a consistently healthy starting quarterback. Jimmy Garoppolo operated the offense efficiently as it averaged almost 30 points per game. He was not built to be a quarterback who puts the game on his shoulders. He was built to keep the chains moving. He did so, splendidly.

Second lesson learned: Seattle can spoil happiness. The Seahawks ended the 49ers' winning streak in a Week 10 Monday night game. The Niners kicked a late field goal to force overtime. In a frustrating extra period, ending in a tie seemed likely until Seattle quarterback (and 49er nemesis) Russell Wilson drove his team to a winning field goal as the overtime clock expired.

Third lesson learned: Defense can be a happy way to win, too. The 49ers' unit ranked second in the league in total defense and first in passing defense. Defensive Rookie of the Year Nick Bosa definitely helped. So did Arik Armstead's 10 sacks. So did adding cornerback Richard Sherman. So did a shutdown linebacker festival organized by Fred Warner and Dre Greenlaw.

Fourth lesson learned: Proper tackling form counts. The last game of the NFL's 100th season was purposely scheduled to highlight a longtime rivalry. The division title and No. 1 playoff seed were on the line at Seattle's CenturyLink Field, where the 49ers were riding an eight-game losing streak.

The Niners led 26–21 with nine seconds remaining. Seattle's offense faced fourth and goal at the 5-yard line. Wilson flipped a pass to tight end Jacob Hollister. Greenlaw met him with perfect technique and dropped him inches short of the end zone.

"I just made sure that my feet were on the goal line and played lateral to downhill," Greenlaw said, "and I made a tackle that my coaches and teammates would be proud of. Just happy with how the game ended and happy to be able to make the play."[178]

For the first time under Kyle Shanahan, the 49ers resembled the Scarlet Heroes of Yore.

Kansas City Chiefs quarterback Patrick Mahomes attempts a pass over the hands of Nick Bosa during Super Bowl LIV.
COURTESY OF NHAT V. MEYER/MEDIANEWS GROUP/*THE MERCURY NEWS* VIA GETTY IMAGES

Super Bowl LIV: A Three-Quarters Champion

IN THE same Miami stadium where Joe Montana had led his famous comeback and Steve Young had lost his monkey, the 49ers sought to complete their amazing reversal of a season with a Super Bowl title. They had easily dispatched the Green Bay Packers in the NFC Championship Game, 37–20. The only hurdle left was a Kansas City Chiefs team with its wunderkind quarterback, Patrick Mahomes.

As 49ers coach Kyle Shanahan did his game planning, he looked at the Chiefs' high-powered offense and had a tough strategic decision to make. As much as he loved Jimmy Garoppolo's steady efficiency, Shanahan knew it would be folly to get in a shootout with Mahomes, in only his third NFL season but an All Pro and league MVP. The 49ers coach played a conservative hand. He took few risks, used up clock on long drives, settled for field goals, utilized Deebo Samuel effectively as a runner and receiver, and relied on the Niners' defense to slow down the Chiefs. The plan succeeded. After three quarters, the 49ers were Super Bowl champions. They had a 10-point lead with eight minutes remaining. Mahomes had not completed a pass longer than 13 yards and had been intercepted twice.

Alas, the game lasted four quarters. In a finger-snap, everything went wrong. Mahomes completed a 44-yard bomb to Tyreek Hill that led to a touchdown with 6:13 left. After a 49er three-and-out, Mahomes hit a 38-yarder to set up another Chiefs touchdown. The Niners were now behind 24–20. Garoppolo drove the offense to midfield with 1:40 remaining but threw three incompletions before being sacked on fourth down. Kansas City scored again and won the game 31–20.

"We didn't take our opportunities," said tight end George Kittle. "I could give you every cliché in the book—we just didn't get it done."[179]

Lamenting the Niners' shot at immortality, defensive lineman Arik Armstead said: "Nobody remembers the loser."[180]

In this case, that wasn't true. Not after such a collapse. The defeat didn't wipe out everything that the 2019 Niners had achieved. It just deposited a ton of "what ifs" on the season's final eight minutes.

San Francisco quarterback Jimmy Garoppolo looks to pass against the Kansas City Chiefs during Super Bowl LIV.
COURTESY OF TOM PENNINGTON/GETTY IMAGES

The elusive Deebo Samuel zigzags around Los Angeles Rams cornerback Jalen Ramsey for a touchdown.

COURTESY OF THEARON W. HENDERSON/ GETTY IMAGES

Another Dose of Aaron Rodgers Kryptonite

SIX WEEKS after the 49ers' Super Bowl loss in Miami, the COVID pandemic smacked the entire world upside the head and put the defeat in perspective. When a vaccine was developed in the autumn, Levi's Stadium was transformed into a mass inoculation facility. A ban on group gatherings sent the 49ers to Arizona for home games in the Cardinals' State Farm Stadium. With mounting injuries to key players, the 2020 Niners limped to a 6–10 record. Would 2021 be a bounce back or an ugly retreat?

After eight games, ugliness was winning. The 49ers were 3–5 and lacked focus, energy, spunk, and any other noun in the vicinity of "playoff ready." The front office had made a bold move in the draft by trading up to pick Trey Lance, a physical specimen of a quarterback who had played just 19 college games at North Dakota State. They threw him into the fire in Week 5 at Arizona when Garoppolo was hurt. Lance's first pass was intercepted. The Niners lost 17–10.

Stunningly, they found a path out of the mess. Garoppolo returned. Big plays were big played. Tackles were tackled. The Niners finished 10–7 in the NFL's new 17-game format. In the Wild Card playoff game, they upset Dallas 23–17. Their next opponents were the top-seeded Packers in Green Bay, where the forecast was for 14-degree weather with a 30 percent chance of snow and a 100 percent chance of Aaron Rodgers, which was the bigger problem.

Or was it? Rodgers had lost three straight playoff games to the 49ers. For all of his MVP awards and Pro Bowls, the Niners had been his kryptonite. And they were again. Amidst snow flurries, San Francisco muscled out a 13–10 comeback victory. The only 49ers touchdown was scored on a blocked punt returned to the end zone by rookie Talanoa Hufanga. That tied the score with 4:41 remaining. Rodgers came on with another chance to break his 49ers curse. He managed only a 4-yard completion in four downs. The Packers punted. They never got the ball back. Robbie Gould kicked a 45-yard field goal as time expired. Rodgers became the first quarterback in NFL history to lose four playoff games to a single opponent.

The following week, the 49ers lost to the Los Angeles Rams in the NFC title game, 20–17. If only Rodgers had been playing quarterback for the Rams.

Talanoa Hufanga celebrates after returning a blocked punt for a touchdown at a snowy playoff game against the Green Bay Packers in January 2022.

COURTESY OF MICHAEL ZAGARIS/SAN FRANCISCO 49ERS/GETTY IMAGES

Attention Grabbers and Gravity Centers

QUARTERBACKS AND receivers are the attention centers in the NFL. For good reason. Deebo Samuel's knockdown running and pass-catching style juiced up the 49ers as they moved through the Shanahan era. Whether he lined up as a receiver or in the backfield, he was nearly impossible to tackle. Samuel explained: "You've got to have that dog in you, having that mindset of not one person is going to bring you down."[181]

On defense, the attention centers are usually pass rushers like Nick Bosa. The 49ers acquired him out of Ohio State with the No. 2 pick in 2019 draft. He terrorized opposing quarterbacks to earn Defensive Player of the Year honors in 2023. Bosa then became the highest paid defensive player in NFL history.

But for winning football teams, attention centers are not as important as gravity centers. They're the players that other players look to for setting a standard or holding people accountable. As the 49ers constructed their Super Bowl contending teams of the 2020s, two centers of gravity surfaced organically.

Trent Williams, a 6-foot-5, 320-pound offensive tackle, was a blocking force of some repute when the 49ers obtained him from Washington in a 2020 trade. He proudly wore his nickname of "Silverback," after the male gorilla, as a back tattoo. But his overall influence was even more weighty than the Niners imagined. He gained an entire roster's respect with his skill and bearing. Teammates touted Williams as the league's top player. At any position.

"Trent's the best player in the NFL, for sure. No doubt," said linebacker Dre Greenlaw after facing Williams every day in practice. "If he's not the best player, he's one of the best athletes. Especially for that size. It's just ridiculous."[182]

Fred Warner could be called ridiculous in another sense. A third-round draft choice out of Brigham Young in 2018 who made zero All-American teams, Warner spent two years honing his NFL chops with maniacal iPad video study and demonic gym sessions, molding himself into an All-Pro linebacker and defensive captain.

"I always think about what I can do better," Warner said. "I'm pretty hard on myself. . . If you want to be a great player in this league, it takes those everyday things leading up to the game. It takes preparing day in and day out, and doing the little things right."[183]

Bosa concurred: "He's a great leader. He gets our mind right whenever we need it."[184]

Which is a pretty good definition of a gravity center.

Linebacker Nick Bosa (left) and offensive tackle Trent Williams demonstrate two types of dominant players on the 49ers roster.

COURTESY OF RYAN KAN (*WILLIAMS*) AND THEARON W. HENDERSON (*BOSA*)/GETTY IMAGES

Fred Warner fires up the team before the NFC Divisional playoff game against the Dallas Cowboys in January 2023.

COURTESY OF MICHAEL ZAGARIS/SAN FRANCISCO 49ERS/GETTY IMAGES

Instant Christian: McCaffrey Returns to the Bay with Immediate Results

"IT'S A surreal moment for me," said Christian McCaffrey when he walked into the 49ers' locker room for the first time.[185]

Two weeks earlier, McCaffrey had been wearing a Carolina Panthers uniform. He was playing against the 49ers, trying to beat them. Now, he was supposed to carry the ball for them across the Super Bowl goal line. At Stanford, McCaffrey had taken the Cardinal to major heights as an All-American back and Heisman Trophy runner-up. After he became a Pro Bowl mainstay with the Panthers, however, seeing him back in the Bay wasn't on anyone's Bingo card.

Yet here McCaffrey was at Levi's Stadium in October 2022, literally ready to hit the ground running after a blockbuster midseason deal. It had become the First Law of Lynch and Shanahan: When in doubt, never doubt that a big-impact trade will happen. This time, the coach and general manager gave up four valuable high draft picks for McCaffrey.

The 49ers badly needed him after another mediocre start. Six weeks into the season, they were 3–3 and banged up at many positions. Their ground game was dormant. Second-year quarterback Trey Lance had been the starter until he was injured in Week 2. Jimmy Garoppolo—himself on the trading block in the offseason until no worthy offers surfaced—was not performing well out of the bullpen. McCaffrey's arrival was greeted warmly by all hands. "It's a shot in the arm," said offensive tackle Trent Williams.[186]

The surprise was how quickly the shot took effect. Just three days after arriving in Santa Clara, McCaffrey played 21 snaps against the Kansas City Chiefs. He ripped off 9-yard and 10-yard runs on his first two carries to wild applause. The 49ers lost the game. But everyone could see the possibilities. The 49ers did not lose another game until January. They spooled out 10 straight victories to finish the regular season, in large part due to the McCaffrey effect. Using his athleticism in Week 8 against the Rams, he became only the 11th player in NFL history to produce passing, rushing, and receiving touchdowns in the same game.

Significantly, McCaffrey accomplished this without major wounds or pain, despite his full-tilt running style of reading blocks with micro-pauses before accelerating through gaps and often initiating contact. Could he keep accelerating through the playoffs? The 49ers were counting on it.

The 49ers' midseason trade for running back Christian McCaffrey added a new dimension to the offense.
COURTESY OF COOPER NEILL/ GETTY IMAGES

2022

Mr. Irrelevant to the Rescue

IN 1976, a former 49ers wide receiver from the 1950s named Paul Salata thought it would be fun to honor the player who was the last selection of the NFL draft. Salata and some friends organized an annual weeklong "celebration" in Newport Beach, California, honoring the final round's final man. Salata came up with a nifty nickname for the honoree: Mr. Irrelevant.[187] Forty-six years later, the 49ers owned that last pick. General manager John Lynch got on the phone a few minutes before the official selection and called Iowa State quarterback Brock Purdy. "I'm sorry it took to the end," Lynch said. "We find you very relevant. But you are going to be Mr. Irrelevant."

At training camp, Purdy was slotted as the 49ers' fourth-string quarterback, or maybe a practice squad player. He wasn't that tall, barely 6-foot-1. His arm wasn't a cannon. But it was obvious that Purdy's 48 games as an Iowa State starter were an asset. He had seen a lot. Nothing surprised or confused him. He was impressive in preseason games and in the quarterbacks meeting room with position coach Brian Griese. Mr. Irrelevant survived all the roster cuts and wound up third on the depth chart.

He moved up to No. 2 after Trey Lance suffered a broken ankle and was replaced by Jimmy Garoppolo. Then Jimmy G broke his foot in the first quarter against the Dolphins. Purdy stepped up in the 33–17 win. He was now No. 1. His first NFL start was against the Tampa Bay Buccaneers, merely quarterbacked by Tom Brady, winner of seven Super Bowls. Purdy non-nervously threw two TD passes with no interceptions and rushed for a score in a 35–7 Niners victory. Walking off the field, Brady congratulated Purdy and left him a little speechless.

"I'm not going to lie," Purdy said. "Being a little kid and watching that guy kill it throughout those years . . . For him to have respect for what I did, it was pretty cool."[188]

Purdy went 5–0 as a starter the rest of the season. Sadly, Paul Salata had died 14 months earlier, before he could witness what the greatest Mr. Irrelevant of all time had wrought.

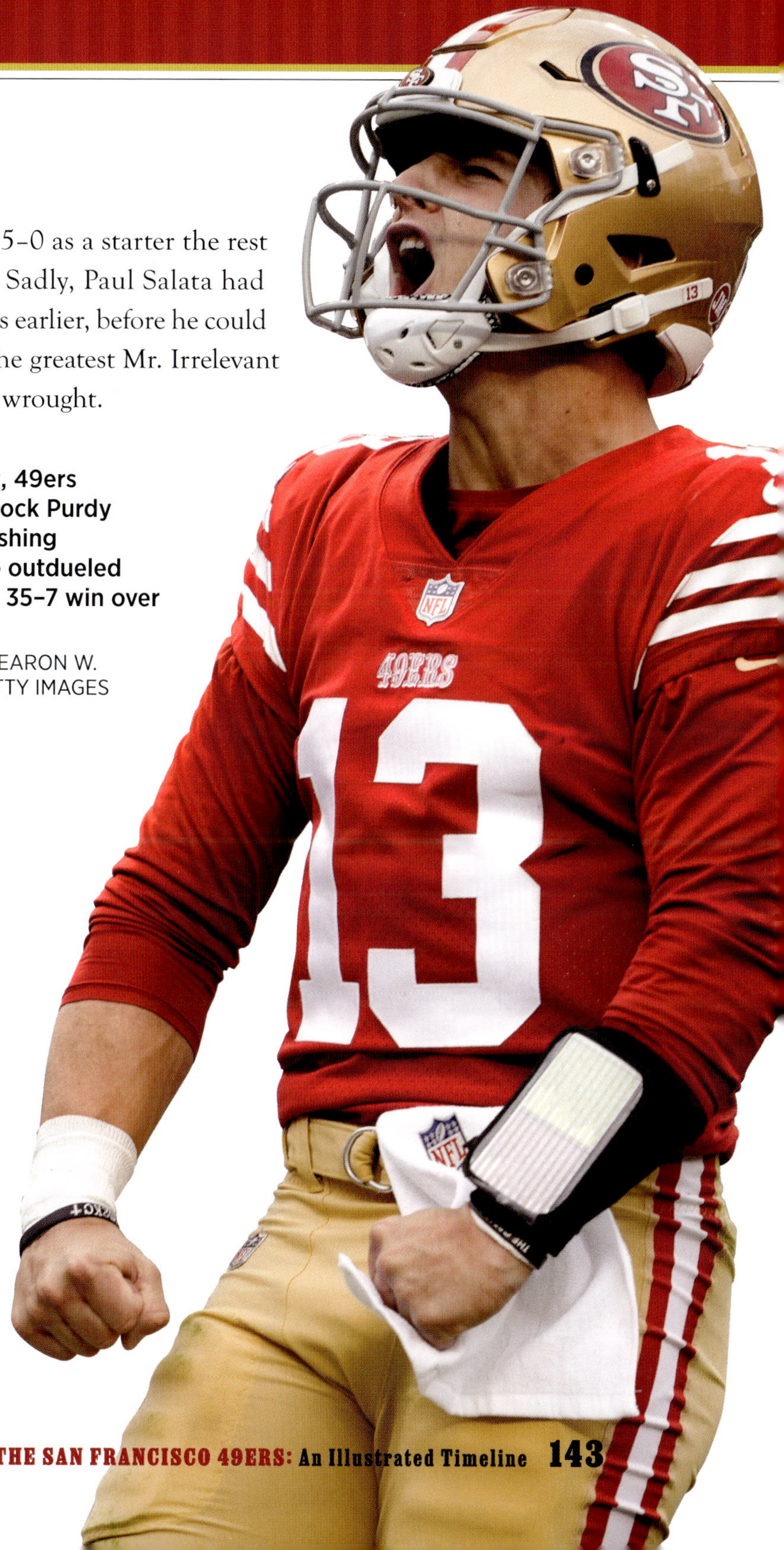

In his first start, 49ers quarterback Brock Purdy celebrates a rushing touchdown. He outdueled Tom Brady in a 35–7 win over Tampa Bay.

COURTESY OFTHEARON W. HENDERSON/GETTY IMAGES

The Super Bowl Express Crashes in Philly

THE 49ERS were on a roll. After they lucked into Brock Purdy being the best rookie quarterback the franchise had ever seen (Joe Montana didn't start until his second season), they rototillered themselves to a 13–4 record. Then they made quick work of Seattle in the Wild Card playoff round, 41–23, as Purdy threw three TD passes (and ran for another, just because he could).

The game's most-replayed highlight was a short pass to Deebo Samuel that he converted into a spectacular 74-yard touchdown. The most replayed reaction shot was of Purdy pounding his chest and screaming to the sky after an improvised fourth-quarter TD pass.

"I love seeing him let his emotion out like that," said 49ers fullback Kyle Juszczyk, "because he's a pretty calm, cool, collected guy—not very loud. But when he lets it out, it fires you up."[189]

The following Sunday featured more Purdy ad-lib theater against the Dallas Cowboys. In the fourth quarter of a defensive struggle, as pressure closed in, he caught sight of George Kittle going rogue to an open area. Purdy sent a 30-yard pass in his direction. Kittle juggled it at full speed before hauling it in. Hey diddle diddle, Kittle up the middle. It set up Christian McCaffrey's 2-yard go-ahead TD run in an eventual 19–12 victory.

"Kittle wasn't supposed to run down the field like that but he felt space," Purdy said. "I just have to lead him and hit him. It seemed like it was 10 seconds of bobbling."[190]

"He gave me a catchable ball and I was just trying to be dramatic for TV," Kittle said. "Get the ratings up. That's all we're here for."[191]

Next up was the NFC Championship Game in Philadelphia. The roll was still rolling—until the sixth snap of the Niners' first drive. Eagles pass rusher Hassan Reddick hit Purdy's throwing arm in mid-delivery. Something snapped in his elbow. It was a torn ulnar collateral ligament.

"My arm just felt like it stretched out," Purdy said. "Felt a lot of shocks all over, from my elbow down to my wrist, front and back. Just pain, really, all over."[192]

He gave way to fourth-string quarterback Josh Johnson, who suffered a third-quarter concussion and left the game. Purdy returned to the field but could throw the ball no farther than 10 yards. Final score: Philadelphia 31, Niners 7. The Quest for Six remained stymied at five.

George Kittle uses great concentration to make a juggling catch against Dallas in a 2023 playoff game.

COURTESY OF MICHAEL ZAGARIS/SAN FRANCISCO 49ERS/GETTY IMAGES

Purdy and McCaffrey Make the Scoreboard Sing

WHILE BROCK Purdy rehabbed his repaired elbow in the offseason, the 49ers let Jimmy Garoppolo leave as a free agent to Las Vegas and traded Trey Lance to Dallas. Kyle Shanahan was all in on Purdy, even if Shanahan did consider recruiting just-retired Tom Brady in case Brock wasn't ready when the season started. Purdy had passed on Tommy John surgery that could have sidelined him for a year and chose to fix the elbow with an internal space-age brace. March surgery allowed him to begin throwing footballs in May and be at full go in August. Purdy also told reporters the rehab included naps. Seriously.

"Just getting really good sleep," he said. "I know it sounds cheesy, but that, I think, is a game-changer in terms of getting back from an injury."[193]

Sleepy Brock was Brilliant Brock as the 49ers went undefeated in their first five games. He was also Bargain Brock. The beauty of Purdy's entry contract as a seventh-round pick—with an annual salary-cap hit of less than $1 million through 2024—was that it gave the team oodles of cap space to load up on expensive talent at other positions. Other teams paid their quarterbacks in the eight figures. Bargain Brock was earning six figures.

Both high-salary and low-salary players contributed to the 49ers' Week 5 thumping of Dallas, 42–10, on *Sunday Night Football*. Purdy threw four TD passes, three to George Kittle. Fred Warner intercepted a pass, forced a fumble deep in Dallas territory, and sacked Dak Prescott.

Other than during a three-week losing streak, it was full Christian McCaffrey ahead for the 49ers. The running back continued his remarkable hard-charging consistency and tied Lenny Moore's 58-year-old NFL record with touchdowns in 17 consecutive games. McCaffrey then nearly broke the record in a 34–3 romp over Jacksonville but couldn't catch up to a third-down pass in the fourth quarter that would have done it.

"I suck," McCaffrey wisecracked. "Everyone else on the team scored. Except me."[194]

By season's end, Purdy had thrown for 4,280 yards, setting a franchise record and surpassing Montana, Young, Garcia, Kaepernick, Brodie, and all the rest. In a Week 11 win over Tampa Bay, Purdy attained a perfect 158.3 passer rating by going 21-for-25 for 333 yards, three touchdowns, and zero interceptions.

"Brock reminds me a lot of Montana. His coolness. He doesn't get rattled," Jerry Rice told Fred Warner on *The Warner House* podcast. "You need your quarterback to be that way."[195]

Brock Purdy set the 49er franchise record with 4,280 passing yards in 2023, along with 31 touchdown passes.
COURTESY OF MICHAEL OWENS/ GETTY IMAGES

In a 2023 rematch against the Philadelphia Eagles, Deebo Samuel exploded for three touchdowns.
COURTESY OF RYAN KANG/GETTY IMAGES

December 3, 2023

Deebo Dumps a Bucket of Revenge on Philadelphia

THERE WAS nothing subtle about the buildup for the anticipated Week 13 rock fight between the 49ers and Philadelphia Eagles. Some people speculated that Philly fans would bring actual rocks to Lincoln Financial Field.

The game was a settling of scores. On both sides. Eleven months earlier, in the NFC title game with a Super Bowl trip at stake, the 49ers had been hammered by the Eagles after losing quarterback Brock Purdy on their first offensive series. Deebo Samuel was among many 49ers convinced that they would have won otherwise. The Eagles were convinced that Samuel and those many 49ers were pouting whiners.

"We lost that playoff game because we played with 10 people," Samuel had said in the offseason.[196]

"It was a lot of boo-hoos last year, a lot of crying, a lot of what if," said Eagles linebacker Haason Reddick, whose hit had imploded Purdy's elbow. "They get a chance to come back in here, line that (expletive) up again and prove it."[197]

The 49ers complied. They poured a bucket of revenge on the Eagles, 42–19, with Samuel as the bucket supervisor. It was almost laughable to watch. He drowned Philadelphia with three touchdowns, one on a 15-yard lateral and the other two on pass receptions of 48 and 46 yards. After a slow first quarter, the Niner offense scored touchdowns on six consecutive possessions. The defense had a very effective bad attitude. Linebacker Dre Greenlaw's sideline suplex tackle resulted in a shove from the nearby Eagles' security chief, who in return was poked in the face by Greenlaw. Both men were ejected. Christian McCaffrey had 93 yards rushing and finished off the beatdown with a late touchdown.

"Obviously, we wanted some payback," said Nick Bosa.[198]

The Eagles had entered the game with the NFC's best record (10–1). The 49ers were two games behind (8–3). Afterward, the gap had narrowed and the Niners would go on to finish 12–5 and earn the No. 1 seed in the playoffs. In another subplot, Purdy and Eagles quarterback Jalen Hurts were midseason league MVP candidates and their matchup was advertised as a barometer of their chances. Purdy threw for 314 yards with four touchdowns and no interceptions for a 148.8 passer rating. Hurts had 298 yards, one touchdown, and an 85.2 rating.

The 49ers' plane ride back to the Bay served no boo-hoos.

The Purdy Packer Comeback

IT IS settled policy among the 49er Faithful. To gain official clutch quarterback status and be remembered fondly forever, a candidate must lead a thrilling comeback in the final minutes of a big playoff game and pull out an improbable victory. For all of Brock Purdy's feats during his rapid rise to Niner fame and his superior 2023 season, he had never done that. Until January 20, 2024.

But with 6:21 left in the fourth quarter of the 49ers' first playoff game, things weren't looking too ducky. Unless you were a duck. Rain was falling like a son of a blitzer. The Green Bay Packers were ready to kick a 41-yard field goal and add to their 21–17 lead at Levi's Stadium. But the field goal was no good. Purdy and the 49er offense would have one last chance to go 69 yards and win the game.

"Hey guys," Purdy told the huddle. "Lock in."[199]

This was a rather audacious command, given that Purdy had been sloshing through an uninspired afternoon on 17-of-32 passing. He had unlocked almost no big plays, save a 32-yard second-quarter TD pass to George Kittle. The underdog Packers' unheralded quarterback, Jordan Love, was outplaying Purdy. And the 49ers were without the injured Deebo Samuel.

Eleven plays later, Mr. Irrelevant had completed six of seven pass attempts for 47 yards, had gained 11 yards on two carries, and had driven his team to the 6-yard line, where he handed off the ball to Christian McCaffrey for a go-ahead touchdown with 1:07 remaining. After the Packers' final possession, when a frantic Love threw an interception to Dre Greenlaw, the final score was as locked in as Brock: Niners 24, Packers 17.

"Obviously it's four quarters for a reason, you know?" Purdy said. "So the way I started, it's like, 'Man, I've got to be better, got to play efficient football.' But when it comes down to it, with the season on the line, you've got to make it happen for your boys around you."[200]

Jauan Jennings climbs the ladder for a key reception against the Packers in the 2023 playoffs.
COURTESY OF THEARON W. HENDERSON/GETTY IMAGES

"What a win," said defensive captain Fred Warner. "I feel exhausted. That took everything. It took everyone."[201]

No kidding. Among the craziest moments in the winning drive was a 17-yard catch by Chris Conley, who had been cut by the Niners in the preseason and had three total receptions after rejoining the team. The 49ers were full of surprise heroes as they advanced to the NFC title game.

Brock Purdy uses his legs to gain key yardage in the 49ers' 17-point comeback in the NFC Championship Game against the Detroit Lions.

COURTESY OF MICHAEL ZAGARIS/SAN FRANCISCO 49ERS/GETTY IMAGES

January 28, 2024

A Ladybug Luck Rally Spectacular

THE LADYBUG did not have a ticket or field pass. It still somehow made its way to the Levi's Stadium turf before the game, during warmups. The ladybug landed on the shoe of 49ers wide receiver Brandon Aiyuk. "Y'all know what that means," Aiyuk would say later.[202]

Ladybugs mean good luck, if you believe in superstition. And this particular ladybug meant that, a few hours later, Aiyuk would make a freaky-deaky holy-cannoli play that pivoted the momentum 180 degrees and spurred the 49ers' revival from a 24–7 halftime deficit to defeat the Detroit Lions 34–31 and earn a trip to Super Bowl LVIII. "That was the play that changed things," said 49er fullback Kyle Juszczyk. "It was on after that."[203]

Before that? It was off. And awful. The Lions could do nothing wrong in the first half, and the 49ers did nothing much to stop them. Three different Detroit running backs scored touchdowns. Lions quarterback Jared Goff was cool and in control, building a 17-point lead.

About the 49ers' locker room at halftime, Brock Purdy said, "No one was rah-rah. No one was freaking out. It was football. There's enough veterans on this team that have been in crazy situations and it was, 'We have to do our job. Straight up.'"[204]

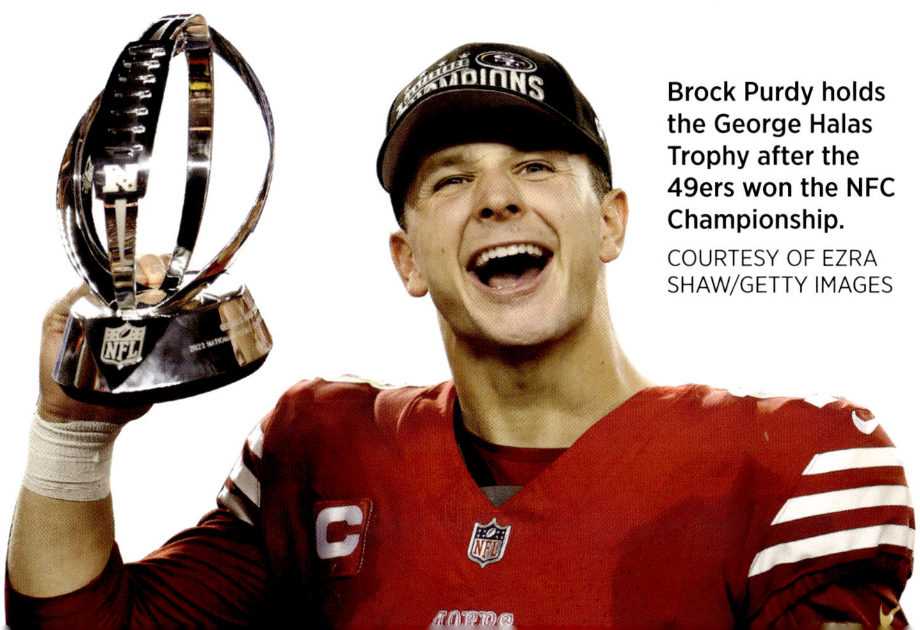

Brock Purdy holds the George Halas Trophy after the 49ers won the NFC Championship.

COURTESY OF EZRA SHAW/GETTY IMAGES

Niners wide receiver Brandon Aiyuk catches a pass that bounced off of Lions defender Kindle Vildor in the NFC Championship Game.

COURTESY OF EZRA SHAW/GETTY IMAGES

That included the ladybug. Midway through the third quarter the 49ers were trailing 24–10 when Purdy sailed the football 50 yards toward Aiyuk at the Lions' 10-yard line. Aiyuk was slowed down by Detroit cornerback Kindle Vildor, who reached up to grab the pass. The ball slipped through Vildor's arms and then—huh?—bounced off his face mask. Aiyuk kept his eyes on the ball and dove to snatch it from the air before he landed at the 4-yard line.

"When I saw him catch that," Purdy said. "I was like, 'That's insane.'"[205]

It got zanier. Three plays after Aiyuk's grab, the Lions led by just 24–17. Ladybug luck continued. On the Lions' next possession, running back Jahmyr Gibbs mishandled the ball and 49er lineman Arik Armstead fell on it at the Detroit 24. After Purdy's 21-yard scramble, Christian McCaffrey scored and the game was tied. Lions coach Dan Campbell twice went for it on fourth down instead of kicking field goals, and twice they fell short. Meanwhile, Purdy's scrambling and McCaffrey's power running set up 10 more points to ensure a Niners victory. Another week, another comeback. This one tied the 2012 team for the largest comeback in NFC Championship history.

Maybe the 49ers weren't America's team. But they were the Entomologists' Team. Do NFC-title T-shirts come in Ladybug sizes?

February 11, 2024

Super Bowl LVIII: Sin City and Kansas City

THE FIRST Super Bowl to be played in Las Vegas was always going to be a big deal. Pun intended. When the matchup was firmed up as the 49ers vs. the Kansas City Chiefs, the big deal doubled down. Kansas City was the defending NFL champion with the league's consensus best quarterback, Patrick Mahomes. The 49ers featured the NFL Offensive Player of the Year, Christian McCaffrey. Meanwhile, Kansas City tight end Travis Kelce was dating the world's biggest pop star, Taylor Swift. And the wife of 49ers fullback Kyle Juszczyk was making custom jackets for Taylor Swift. You couldn't make this stuff up.

Nor could anyone forget the game's most obvious angle: It was a rematch of Super Bowl LIV, when the 49ers were ahead 20–10 with eight minutes left in the game and blew the lead as Mahomes led the Chiefs to three late touchdowns. The eight 49er players who were part of that game and still on the roster didn't even try to pretend they'd forgotten about it.

"You develop these scars, losing a Super Bowl, losing NFC Championship Games," said Fred Warner. "I think those adversities make you who you are as a team and an individual and harden you for moments like this."[206]

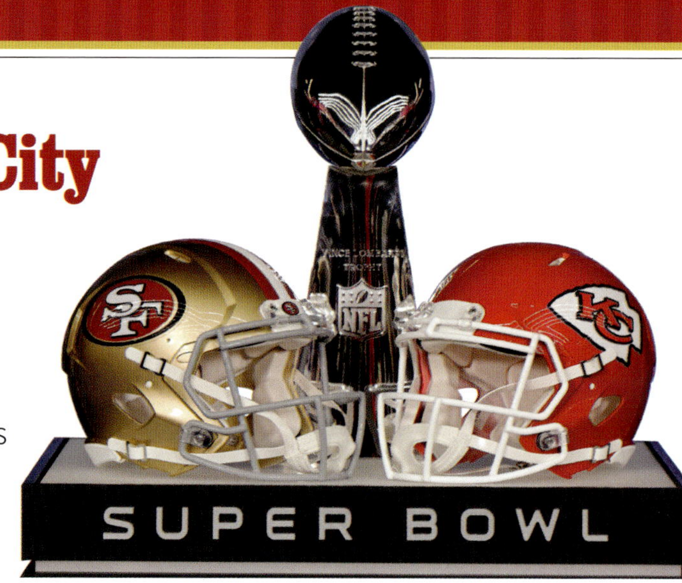

COURTESY OF ETHAN MILLER/GETTY IMAGES

Nick Bosa concurred: "We have to make it count this time."[207]

Most football analysts picked the Chiefs to win, but the sharpies believed the 49ers could. In the casino sports books, the Niners were one and a half point favorites. Despite Kansas City's status as defending champs, the Chiefs were considered vulnerable. Their 2023 regular season had been bumpy. In mid-December, they owned an 8–5 record before making a strong push to finish 11–6 and win the AFC West. Above all, they still had Mahomes, who between filming his several dozen TV commercials found time to remain the NFL's most dangerous man.

"The play is never dead with him," said John Lynch, the 49ers' general manager, assessing his fears. "He can play in rhythm. He can extend. You think you have him tackled and the next thing you know, he's spun out . . . I've got a lot of really painful memories, things that keep you up at night, things that fuel you about that last experience."[208]

The FOM (Fear of Mahomes) Syndrome would be justified. Once more.

The 49ers celebrate after winning the NFC Championship Game against the Detroit Lions. From left, Christian McCaffrey, George Kittle, Deebo Samuel, Trent Williams, Fred Warner, and Brock Purdy.

COURTESY OF MICHAEL ZAGARIS/SAN FRANCISCO 49ERS/GETTY IMAGES

Christian McCaffrey celebrates scoring a touchdown on a pass from 49ers receiver Jauan Jennings in Super Bowl LVIII.
COURTESY OF RYAN KANG/GETTY IMAGES

Kansas City Chiefs quarterback Patrick Mahomes escapes from Nick Bosa in Super Bowl LVIII.

COURTESY OF ETHAN MILLER/GETTY IMAGES

February 11, 2024

Super Bowl LVIII: That Mahomes Guy, Again

COME ON. It couldn't happen again. Could it? It could. The 49ers had a 10-point lead in Super Bowl LVIII. But Patrick Mahomes brought the Kansas City Chiefs back to win. Same as four years earlier.

The final score was Chiefs 25, Niners 22, Mistakes Too Many. The San Francisco litany of errors was shocking and wide ranging. Christian McCaffrey fumbled. A punt return was botched into a turnover. An extra point attempt was blocked. Trent Williams committed multiple penalties. Other chances were missed. Brock Purdy accepted blame, although he didn't play horribly (255 yards, a touchdown, zero picks). And the last three drives Purdy led ended with points that put the 49ers ahead, including a field goal in overtime. He was still mad at himself.

"At the end of the day, we have the offense to score touchdowns and I failed to put the team in position to do that," Purdy said. "For us not to do anything with those opportunities, that's what hurts."[209]

Mahomes hurt them most. Even when the 49ers led by double digits, there was a sense that Mahomes would be ready to pounce and prevail whenever the need arose. In the final two minutes, he finessed an 11-play, 64-yard drive to set up a game-tying field goal and force the OT.

The 49ers won the coin toss and took the ball first. On third down at Kansas City's 9-yard line, a missed assignment left Chiefs sack specialist Chris Jones unblocked and Purdy had to rush a pass for an incompletion. The 49ers settled for a field goal. Mahomes then moved the Chiefs 75 yards for a touchdown to end the game.

Postgame chatter centered almost obsessively on Kyle Shanahan's decision to receive the ball after winning the overtime coin flip. Overtime rules for the playoffs had changed in 2022, and this was the first time they were used. It caused confusion about the proper strategy. Under the new rules, both teams were guaranteed one possession. If the teams were tied after those two possessions, sudden death ensued.

"We went through all the analytics," Shanahan said. "We wanted the ball third. If both teams matched and scored, we wanted to be the ones who had a chance to go win. We got that field goal, so we knew we had to hold them to at least a field goal. If we did, then we thought it was in our hands after that."[210]

The chatter was moot. Whether the odds are better to kick or receive first in overtime, a team must execute. Either way, the 49ers had to stop Mahomes. In Super Bowls, they still haven't.

Brock Purdy throws under pressure from Chiefs defenders in Super Bowl LVIII.
COURTESY OF JAMIE SQUIRE/GETTY IMAGES

Head coach Kyle Shanahan ponders the 49ers' future.
COURTESY OF MICHAEL ZAGARIS/SAN FRANCISCO 49ERS/GETTY IMAGES

2024

The Never-Ending Niners Mojo

HOW YOU feel about the 49ers' future likely depends on whether you see Kyle Shanahan's scraggly beard as half-grown or half-shaved.

Do you applaud because in the past five years under Shanahan, only the Kansas City Chiefs have appeared in more Super Bowls? Or do you grumble because the Niners have failed to fulfill their Quest for Six after twice blowing fourth-quarter leads in the NFL's ultimate game? The answer is that you do both. No law requires that a favorite sports team be either the best in the world or the worst piece of mascot manure in existence. But in today's cacophony of sports-talk shows, podcasts, blogs, and social media spit-fests, those two viewpoints are the only ones permitted.

Back in the pre-cacophony days, passionate 49er fans hoped for sweet victories but seemed to more easily laugh off bad losses. The 49ers have produced many of both. And very few of those games have been dull. For this, the 49er Faithful should be grateful. Throughout nearly eight decades of existence, the franchise has developed a certain genetic code of innovative coaches, stylish running backs, soap-opera quarterback controversies, foggy nights, hard-hitting defensive backs, charismatic receivers, and ultra-competitive Italian American owners. It is how a football team has managed to transfix millions while reaching eight Super Bowls and winning five of them.

Odds are, the mojo will continue, with Brock Purdy as the franchise quarterback and Shanahan and John Lynch on long-term contracts.

In early 2024, Jed York officially became the 49ers' principal owner. And in a shocking development, he backtracked on his statement about the 49ers wanting NFL championship banners or nothing.

"You can't be ashamed of a successful season," York said. "Our goal is always going to be to win Super Bowls. . . . What I've learned in my time as CEO, it's not a complete failure to not win. . . . The only way to win the Super Bowl is you have to get there first. And we've obviously been very close several times. You have to keep building off it. It almost seems worse to lose a Super Bowl than to not make the playoffs, and I don't think that's how teams should feel."[211]

That is a remarkably healthy perspective. Not sure what Tony Morabito or Eddie DeBartolo would think of it. But, if this book proves anything, it is that there should be an appreciation for what has gone before in relation to what's ahead. It's also okay to gripe about third-down play-calling. That's been going on at 49er games since 1946, in a distinct Bay Area manner, unlike anything or anywhere else. That won't ever change. Thank goodness. Forget alleged Northern California sophistication. When's the next kickoff?

The 49er Faithful in 1990 were accustomed to winning championships.
COURTESY OF DAVID MADISON/GETTY IMAGES

Joe Montana and Brent Jones in the locker room before a 1990 game.

COURTESY OF MICHAEL ZAGARIS

ENDNOTES

1 Author interview with Al Ruffo, June 2001.
2 Jason Turbow, "West Coast brew gave stadium its color," *New York Times*, January 20, 2012.
3 Mark Purdy, "Valley sports figures on the cutting edge," *San Jose Mercury News*, June 20, 2001.
4 Chuck Hildebrand, *Bronco Sundays*, 104.
5 Dave Newhouse, *Founding 49ers: The Dark Days Before the Dynasty*, 17.
6 Joseph Hession, *Forty Niners: 50th Anniversary Collector's Edition*, 52.
7 AAFC statistics are not officially recognized by the NFL.
8 Robert K. Fitts, *Wally Yonamine: The Man Who Changed Japanese Baseball*, 37.
9 Hession, *Forty Niners*, 52.
10 Dave Newhouse, *The Million Dollar Backfield: The San Francisco 49ers in the 1950s*, 19.
11 Newhouse, *Founding 49ers*, 43.
12 Newhouse, *The Million Dollar Backfield*, 23.
13 Quoted in: Hession, *Forty Niners*, 30.
14 Newhouse, *Founding 49ers*, 54.
15 Mike Sando, "NFL 100: At No. 83, Leo Nomellini was bigger than life, and his life was very big," *The Athletic*, July 17, 2021.
16 Matt Maiocco, *San Francisco 49ers: The Complete Illustrated History*, 32.
17 Hession, *Forty Niners*, 34.
18 Harry M. Hayward, "Shaw fired by Morabito," *San Francisco Examiner*, December 14, 1954.
19 Newhouse, *Founding 49ers*, 82.
20 Newhouse, *The Million Dollar Backfield*, 180.
21 Dan McGuire, *San Francisco 49ers*. Quoted in: Dennis Georgatos, *Game of My Life: San Francisco 49ers: Memorable Stories of 49ers Football*, 18.
22 Newhouse, *The Million Dollar Backfield*, 181.
23 Kristine Setting Clark, *St. Clair: I'll Take It Raw!–San Francisco 49er Great and Pro Football Hall of Fame Member Bob St. Clair*, 72.
24 Newhouse, *Founding 49ers*, 98.
25 Dwight Chapin, "Creator of the shotgun," *San Francisco Chronicle*, August 19, 2001.
26 "49ers are trigger happy–Shotgun rips Lions, 49–0," *San Francisco Examiner*, October 2, 1961.
27 Newhouse, *Founding 49ers*, 102.
28 Wells Twombly, "An end to elegance," *San Francisco Examiner*, April 11, 1977.
29 Clark, *St. Clair: I'll Take It Raw!*, 59.
30 Jim J. Campbell, *Total 49ers*, 48.
31 Dan Brown, *100 Things 49ers Fans Should Know and Do Before They Die*, 146.
32 Newhouse, *Founding 49ers*, 128.
33 Ibid., 126.
34 Daniel Brown and Dennis Georgatos, "Ex-49ers coach Dick Nolan dies," *San Jose Mercury News*, November 12, 2007.
35 Newhouse, *Founding 49ers*, 145.
36 John Brodie profile, *Monday Night Magazine*, ESPN.
37 Daniel Brown, "Hall of Fame push for John Brodie," *San Jose Mercury News*, July 30, 2015.
38 Newhouse, *Founding 49ers*, 158.
39 1970 49ers-Vikings playoff postgame radio interviews.
40 Brian Murphy, *San Francisco 49ers From Kezar to Levi's Stadium*, 113.
41 Newhouse, *Founding 49ers*, 172.
42 Ibid., 167.
43 David Harris, *The Genius: How Bill Walsh Reinvented Football and Created an NFL Dynasty*, 14.
44 Ibid., 53.
45 Bill Walsh, Steve Jamison, and Craig Walsh, *The Score Takes Care of Itself: My Philosophy of Leadership*, 43.
46 Harris, *The Genius*, 76.
47 Ibid., 121.
48 Harris, *The Genius*, 14.
49 Paul Zimmerman, "Born to be a quarterback," *Sports Illustrated*, August 6, 1990.
50 "Ronnie Lott: The Hardest Hitting Safety of All Time," *A Football Life*, NFL Films.
51 Brown, *100 Things 49ers Fans Should Know*, 1.
52 1982 49ers-Cowboys NFC Championship Game telecast.
53 Jerry Green, *Super Bowl Chronicles: A Sportswriter Reflects on the First 30 Years of America's Game*, 159.
54 Harris, *The Genius*, 151.
55 Mark Purdy, "Bill Walsh: Ahead of the game," *Cincinnati Enquirer*, January 26, 1982.
56 Jerry Rice and Randy O. Williams, *50 Years, 50 Moments: The Most Unforgettable Plays in Super Bowl History*, 275.
57 Harris, *The Genius*, 178.
58 Art Spander, "In the end, it was the Zebras who had to save the Hogs," *San Francisco Examiner*, January 9, 1984.

59 Harris, *The Genius*, 209.
60 *A Team Above All*, NFL Films.
61 Green, *Super Bowl Chronicles*, 198.
62 Ibid., 198.
63 Brown, *100 Things 49ers Fans Should Know*, 90.
64 Green, *Super Bowl Chronicles*, 198.
65 Mark Purdy, "Super Niners," *San Jose Mercury News*, January 21, 1985.
66 Harris, *The Genius*, 240.
67 Mark Purdy, "Wise Solomon knew Rice would be great one," *San Jose Mercury News*, August 1, 2010.
68 Brown, *100 Things 49ers Fans Should Know*, 29.
69 Roger Craig, Matt Maiocco, and Daniel Brown, *Roger Craig's Tales from the San Francisco 49ers Sideline: A Collection of Greatest 49ers Stories Ever Told*, ix.
70 Harris, *The Genius*, 260.
71 Mark Purdy, "Arms and the man," *West Magazine*, October 28, 1990.
72 Ibid.
73 Mark Purdy, "'88 to measure Walsh's savvy," *San Jose Mercury News*, September 4, 1988.
74 Mark Purdy, "Will QB relays last all season?" *San Jose Mercury News*, September 12, 1988.
75 Lowell Cohn, "No stumblebum in the second half," *San Francisco Chronicle*, October 31, 1988.
76 Brown, *100 Things 49ers Fans Should Know*, 100.
77 Ibid., 100.
78 Mark Purdy, "In Walsh's finest hour, an 'impossible' victory," *San Jose Mercury News*, January 9, 1989.
79 Ibid.
80 Ibid.
81 Green, *Super Bowl Chronicles*, 242.
82 Mark Purdy, "Last gasp: All guts, all glory," *San Jose Mercury News*, January 23, 1989.
83 Adam Lazarus, *Best of Rivals: Joe Montana, Steve Young, and the Inside Story Behind the NFL's Greatest Quarterback Controversy*, 102.
84 Mark Purdy, "Last gasp: All guts, all glory," *San Jose Mercury News*, January 23, 1989.
85 Ibid.
86 Harris, *The Genius*, 341.
87 Jeff Schultz, "Walsh hands off to Seifert," *San Jose Mercury News*, January 27, 1989.
88 Mark Purdy, "Pressure builds on calm Seifert," *San Jose Mercury News*, April 7, 1989.
89 Ron Thomas, "49ers 'DL'–Dissatisfied List–is growing," *San Francisco Chronicle*, September 22, 1989.
90 Paul Zimmerman, "The ultimate winner," *Sports Illustrated*, August 13, 1990.
91 Ron Borges, "Montana ignites the 49ers, 38–28," *Boston Globe*, September 25, 1989.
92 Mark Purdy, "A sudden noise, and a sudden silence," *San Jose Mercury News*, October 23, 1989.
93 Ron Borges, "Young gives team a lift," *Boston Globe*, October 23, 1989.
94 Ric Bucher, "Taylor's feats can't be ignored," *San Jose Mercury News*, December 17, 1989.
95 Mark Purdy, "Niners play well enough," *San Jose Mercury News*, September 18, 1989.
96 Mark Purdy, "It's Walsh time," *San Jose Mercury News*, November 28, 1989.
97 Mike Antonucci, "Rice not intimidated," *San Jose Mercury News*, January 29, 1990.
98 Lazarus, *Best of Rivals*, 121.
99 Brown, *100 Things 49ers Fans Should Know*, 130.
100 Don Pierson, "49ers anything but complacent," *Chicago Tribune*, September 9, 1990.
101 Mark Purdy, "No three peat," *San Jose Mercury News*, January 21, 1991.
102 Brown, *100 Things 49ers Fans Should Know*, 242.
103 "Young signs for $4.5 million," *St. Petersburg Times*, May 4, 1991.
104 Mike Freeman, "Montana fears he's being phased out," *Washington Post*, September 10, 1991.
105 Dennis Georgatos, "Young boldly stakes claim," *San Jose Mercury News*, May 9, 1992.
106 Mark Purdy, "49ers have no choice: Trade Young," *San Jose Mercury News*, May 10, 1992.
107 Mark Purdy, "Young sparkles in loss to Bills," *San Jose Mercury News*, September 14, 1992.
108 Mark Purdy, "Montana was just himself in return," *San Jose Mercury News*, December 29, 1992.
109 Mark Purdy, "Not Young's fault, but he will be blamed," *San Jose Mercury News*, January 18, 1993.
110 Mark Purdy, "Montana plays show and tell," *San Jose Mercury News*, April 9, 1993.
111 Lazarus, *Best of Rivals*, 186.
112 Clark Judge, "Rice, 49ers rewrite history," *San Jose Mercury News*, September 6, 1994.
113 Ibid.
114 Neil Hohlfeld, "Cool Montana, Chiefs ice 49ers," *Houston Chronicle*, September 12, 1994.
115 Paul Zimmerman, "Shoot-out in Kansas City," *Sports Illustrated*, September 19, 1994.
116 Joan Ryan, "Long road to the top," *San Francisco Chronicle*, January 6, 1995.
117 Clark Judge, "49ers upgrade to Prime Time," *San Jose Mercury News*, September 15, 1994.
118 Brown, *100 Things 49ers Fans Should Know*, 271.
119 *America's Game: 1994 49ers*, NFL Films.
120 Brian Murphy, "More bad news for the offensive line," *Santa Rosa Press Democrat*, October 7, 1994.
121 Green, *Super Bowl Chronicles*, 325.
122 *America's Game: 1994 49ers*, NFL Films.

123 Rice, *50 Years, 50 Moments*, 175.
124 Mark Purdy, "Five surprising weeks," *San Jose Mercury News*, December 11, 1995.
125 Mark Purdy, "Rice hurts knee again," *San Jose Mercury News*, December 16, 1997.
126 Mark Purdy, "What a rush!" *San Jose Mercury News*, September 7, 1998.
127 Ibid.
128 Mark Purdy, "Finishing with a kick," *San Jose Mercury News*, October 19, 1998.
129 Clark Judge, "The Catch II," *San Jose Mercury News*, January 4, 1999.
130 John Crumpacker, "Out of miracles," *San Francisco Examiner*, January 10, 1999.
131 Mark Purdy, "Garcia leaves comfort for home," *San Jose Mercury News*, April 7, 1999.
132 Ibid.
133 Dennis Georgatos, "Goodbye and oh, my," *San Jose Mercury News*, December 18, 2000.
134 Ibid.
135 Dennis Georgatos, "Time for goodbye," *San Jose Mercury News*, December 14, 2000.
136 Ibid.
137 Dennis Georgatos, "Goodbye and oh, my," *San Jose Mercury News*, December 18, 2000.
138 Dennis Georgatos, "Owens on the star," *San Jose Mercury News*, September 25, 2000.
139 Mark Purdy, "Victory does little to ease tension," *San Jose Mercury News*, November 5, 2001.
140 Mark Purdy, "Unbelievable," *San Jose Mercury News*, January 6, 2003.
141 Ibid.
142 Ibid.
143 "One Wild Finish," *NFL's Greatest Games*, NFL Films.
144 KPIX CBS San Francisco Bay Area: https://www.facebook.com/watch/?ref=embed_video&v=632777967478154
145 Mark Purdy, "Big stats can't cure Gore's pain," *San Jose Mercury News*, November 27, 2006.
146 Jim Harbaugh press conference, December 28, 2014.
147 Mark Purdy, "A model pro," *San Jose Mercury News*, December 30, 2005.
148 Brown, *100 Things 49ers Fans Should Know*, 56.
149 Mark Purdy, "Jed York is all grown up," *San Jose Mercury News*, January 8, 2011.
150 Brown, *100 Things 49ers Fans Should Know*, 94.
151 Mark Purdy, "Just a victory away from NFC title," *San Jose Mercury News*, January 15, 2012.
152 Ibid.
153 "Alex Smith, 49ers bounce sloppy Saints," ESPN.com News Services, January 15, 2012.
154 Mark Purdy, "Niners have new toy," *San Jose Mercury News*, November 26, 2012.
155 Mark Purdy, "What a rush!" *San Jose Mercury News*, January 13, 2013.
156 Ibid.
157 "Colin Kaepernick sets QB rushing mark as Niners oust Packers," ESPN.com News Services, January 13, 2013.
158 Mark Purdy, "San Francisco 49ers make history, will make more with Super Bowl matchup," *San Jose Mercury News*, January 21, 2013.
159 Mark Purdy, "No shortage of Harbaughs," *San Jose Mercury News*, January 31, 2013.
160 Ibid.
161 Mark Purdy, "Comeback dims in final minutes," *San Jose Mercury News*, February 4, 2013.
162 Ibid.
163 Mark Purdy, "Fantastick farewell," *San Jose Mercury News*, December 24, 2013.
164 Ibid.
165 Mark Purdy, "49ers can't conquer CenturyLink," *San Jose Mercury News*, January 20, 2014.
166 Mark Purdy, "Late lapses in home opening loss," *San Jose Mercury News*, September 15, 2014.
167 Mark Purdy, "Stadium kicks off superlatives," *San Jose Mercury News*, July 18, 2014.
168 https://x.com/JedYork
169 Mark Purdy, "49ers next move better be good," *San Jose Mercury News*, January 5, 2016.
170 Mark Purdy, "49ers start over," *San Jose Mercury News*, January 2, 2017.
171 Steve Wyche, "Colin Kaepernick explains why he sat during national anthem," NFL.com, August 27, 2016.
172 Mark Purdy, "Kaepernick's actions have league flustered," *San Jose Mercury News*, September 7, 2016.
173 "Jed York: Hold me responsible if 49ers don't win Super Bowls," NBC Sports, December 29, 2014.
174 Kate Fagan, "Slogan connects 49ers to new fans," ESPN.com, January 30, 2013.
175 Mark Purdy, "49ers new coach," *San Jose Mercury News*, February 10, 2017.
176 Paul Schwartz, "The one thing you can't criticize Jimmy Garoppolo for," *New York Post*, January 31, 2020.
177 Cam Inman, "Gorgeous George has a beautiful day," Bay Area News Group, December 10, 2018.
178 "49ers win NFC West," Associated Press, December 30, 2019.
179 Cam Inman, "Super start, sour ending," *San Jose Mercury News*, February 3, 2020.
180 Dieter Kurtenbach, "Nobody remembers the loser," *San Jose Mercury News*, February 2, 2020.
181 Cam Inman, "Contrite Bosa starts on the defensive," Bay Area News Group, April 27, 2019.
182 Matt Maiocco, "Why Greenlaw thinks left tackle Williams is NFL's best player," NBC Sports Bay Area, August 1, 2022.

183 Ethan Bauer, “The evolution of Fred Warner,” *Salt Lake City Desert News*, January 18, 2020.

184 Tristi Rodriguez, “Warner hilariously crashes Bosa’s 49ers media availability,” NBC Sports Bay Area, January 25, 2023.

185 Cam Inman, “McCaffrey’s ‘ecstatic’ trade returns him to Bay Area,” *San Jose Mercury News*, October 22, 2022.

186 Ibid.

187 Angelina Martin, “Watch Lynch’s draft call to Purdy that started it all for 49ers QB,” NBC Sports Bay Area, February 3, 2024.

188 Brock Purdy goes off against Tom Brady, Buccaneers for historic win,” Associated Press, *New York Post*, December 21, 2022.

189 “Purdy’s four TDs lead Niners past Seahawks,” Associated Press, January 14, 2023.

190 Cam Inman, “How ’bout them Niners?” *San Jose Mercury News*, January 15, 2023.

191 Ibid.

192 Dieter Kurtenbach, “Not Purdy: Wheels fall off for Niners in crushing loss,” *San Jose Mercury News*, January 30, 2023.

193 Taylor Wirth, “49ers Purdy breaks down recovery process,” NBC Sports Bay Area, July 27, 2023.

194 Nick Wagoner, “Christian McCaffrey’s TD streak ends,” ESPN.com, November 12, 2023.

195 “The Jerry Rice Episode,” *The Warner House* podcast, https://www.youtube.com/watch?v=DSfBA-glLLo

196 Dieter Kurtenbach, “49ers-Eagles to decide NFC team to beat,” *San Jose Mercury News*, December 3, 2023.

197 Ibid.

198 Cam Inman, “Philadelphia beatdown,” Bay Area News Group, December 4, 2023.

199 Dieter Kurtenbach, “Purdy found his form and saved season for Niners,” *San Jose Mercury News*, January 22, 2024.

200 Jason Mastrodonato, “Greenlaw delivers,” Bay Area News Group, January 22, 2024.

201 Ibid.

202 Jason Mastrodonato, “The catch that saved the season,” *San Jose Mercury News*, January 30, 2024.

203 Ibid.

204 Cam Inman, “Unstoppable,” *San Jose Mercury News*, January 29, 2024.

205 “49ers rally from 17 points down,” Associated Press, January 28, 2024.

206 Jerry McDonald, “Vengeance game,” *San Jose Mercury News*, February 9, 2024.

207 Ibid.

208 “Lynch haunted by defeat in Super Bowl LIV,” Staff and Wire Services, Bay Area News Group, February 3, 2024.

209 Super Bowl LVIII postgame interview, NFL Network.

210 Charean Williams, “Kyle Shanahan on receiving kickoff in OT: We wanted the ball third if it went to sudden death,” NBC Sports, February 11, 2024.

211 Grant Cohn, “Jed York: It’s not a complete failure to not win,” *Sports Illustrated* All 49ers, March 27, 2024.

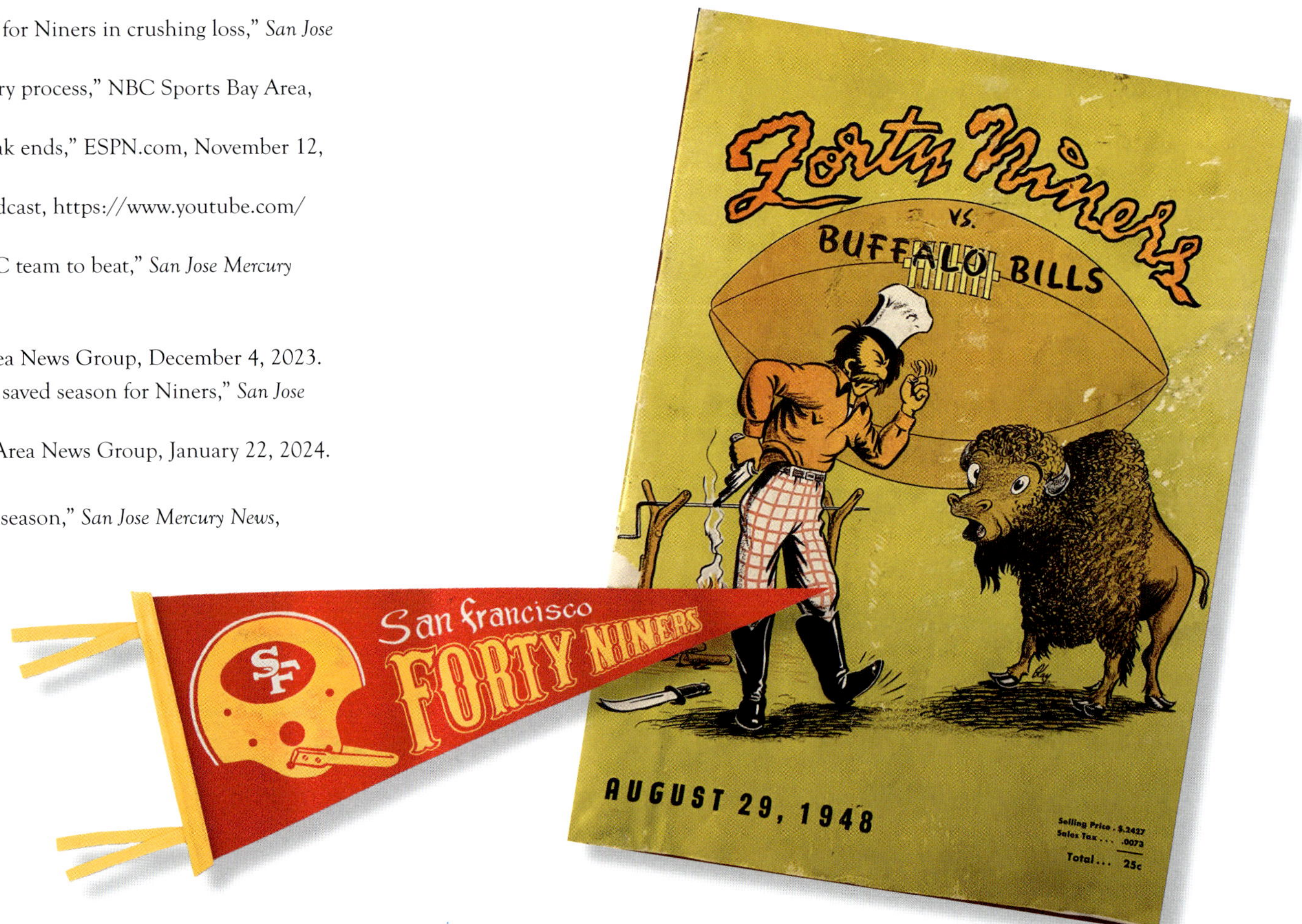

INDEX

49ers Museum, 127
Aikman, Troy, 85
Aiyuk, Brandon, 149
Alameda Naval Air Station, 7
Albert, Frankie, vii, 4, 5, 6, 7, 9, 12, 15, 16, 22
Alexander, Charles, 49
All-America Football Conference (AAFC), 3, 4, 5, 6, 7, 9, 10
Allen, Matt, 111
Alley-Oop, 16, 19
All-Pro, 11, 25, 43, 69, 90, 132, 137, 140
American Football Conference (AFC), 87, 95, 150
American Football League (AFL), 30
Anderson, Ken, 49
Arenas, Joe, 14
Arizona Cardinals, 106, 109, 128, 139
Armstead, Arik, 135, 137, 149
Atlanta Braves, 91
Atlanta Falcons, 28, 30, 79, 82, 91, 98, 103, 121, 124, 132
Atwater Steve, 77
Baalke, Trent, 128
Balboa Park, 6
Baltimore Colts, 10, 22, 35
Baltimore Colts (AAFC), 10, 12
Baltimore Ravens, 122, 123
Banducci, Bruno, 5
Barr, Ron, 36
Barton, Harris, 67, 69, 85
Beals, Alyn, 5, 6, 7, 9
Beathard, C. J., 133, 134
Bergh, Chip, 127
Bono, Steve, 82
Bosa, Nick, 135, 136, 140, 146, 150, 152
Bosley, Bruce, x, 22
Bowman, NaVorro, 124, 125
Boyer, Nate, 129
Brady, Tom, 113, 133, 143, 145
Breech, Jim, 65
Brees, Drew, 118
Breuil, Jim, 7
Brigham Young University (BYU), 61, 83, 140
Brodie, John, vii, 20, 22, 23, 28, 29, 30, 33, 34, 145
Brooklyn Dodgers, 6
Brooks, Ahmad, 127
Brown, Ed, 18
Brown, Jim, 88
Brown, Paul, 9, 10, 36, 49
Brown, Ray, 104
Buffalo Bills, 7, 35, 87, 109, 129
Bunz, Dan, 49
Bush, George H. W., 46
Calgary Stampeders, 106
Campbell, Dan, 149
Canadian League, 12
Candlestick Park, vii, 21, 30, 31, 32, 33, 34, 36, 40, 44, 45, 51, 55, 59, 68, 70, 73, 79, 81, 83, 88, 93, 98, 99, 101, 103, 107, 111, 115, 118, 121, 124, 127
Candy, John, 67
Carmazzi, Giovanni, 113
Carolina Panthers, 98, 125, 142
Carroll, Pete, 117
Carter, Michael, 51, 59
Carter, Virgil, 36
Casanega, Ken, 5
Catch, The, 44, 45, 118
Catch II, The, 103
Catch III, The, 118
Cathcart, Sam, 10
Cavanaugh, Matt, 51
CenturyLink Field, 125, 135
Chicago Bears, 10, 18, 22, 23, 24, 26, 51, 58, 63, 82, 93, 107, 109, 112, 119, 127, 133
Chicago Rockets, 6
Chicago Tribune, 3
Christiansen, Jack, 19, 23, 28
Cincinnati Bengals, ii, 36, 41, 47, 48, 49, 59, 63, 64, 65, 66, 67, 109
Clark, Dwight, 40, 41, 44, 45, 57, 70, 73, 166
Clark, Monte, 34, 35
Clemson University, 41
Cleveland Browns, 6, 9, 10, 13, 14, 19, 22, 33, 68
Cleveland Municipal Stadium, 6
Coach of the Year, 117
Colcicho, Dan, 11
Collinsworth, Cris, 67
Comeback Player of the Year, 116
Conley, Chris, 147
Cooper, Earl, 48
Cosbie, Doug, 45
Cotton Bowl, 37
Cow Palace, 11
Crabtree, Michael, 123, 125
Craig, Roger, 50, 51, 54, 55, 57, 63, 67, 71, 72, 75, 79, 82, 90
Cross, Randy, 35, 62
Cunningham, Randall, 74
Dallas Cowboys, 21, 23, 28, 30, 33, 34, 41, 44, 45, 84, 85, 87, 91, 92, 93, 95, 97, 108, 109, 139, 141, 144, 145
Davis, Al, 35
Davis, Eric, 93
Davis, Vernon, 118
Dean, Fred, 51
DeBartolo, Eddie Jr., vii, 35, 36, 50, 51, 61, 63, 68, 77, 86, 98, 102, 105, 115, 124, 154
DeBartolo, Edward Sr., 35
DeBerg, Steve, 37, 40
Defensive Player of the Year, 91, 140
Delaware State University, 71
Denver Broncos, 76, 77, 78, 99, 132, 134
Detroit Lions, 10, 15, 16, 19, 22, 50, 83, 117, 148, 149, 150
Ditka, Mike, 63
Donahue, Terry, 105, 112
Dorsey, Ken, 113
Eastern Illinois University, 133
Edwards, Edwin, 102
Edwards, Harry, 115
Edwards, Marc, 101
Erickson, Dennis, 112
Eshmont, Len, 6, 8, 87, 116

Esiason, Boomer, 65
Everett, Jim, 71
Faulk, Marshall, 57
Favre, Brett, 98, 103
Fiore, Dave, 104
Floyd, William, 97
Foster, Reuben, 132
Francis, Russ, 51
Freeman, Antonio, 103
Fuller, Jeff, 51, 70
Fuller, Steve, 41
Gabbert, Blaine, 129
Gabriel, Roman, 25
Garcia, Jeff, 104, 106, 109, 111, 113, 116, 145
Garoppolo, Jimmy, 133, 134, 135, 137, 139, 142, 143, 145
Gibbs, Jahmyr, 149
Goff, Jared, 149
Gold Rush cheerleaders, 73, 75
Golden Gate Park, 2, 21, 27
Gonzaga, John, x
Gore, Al, 114
Gore, Frank, 114, 117, 119, 121, 122, 123, 128
Gossett, Bruce, 30
Gould, Robbie, 139
Grab, The, 118
Graham, Corey, 122
Graham, Otto, 6
Grbac, Elvis, 98
Green Bay Packers, 2, 10, 75, 83, 98, 99, 103, 113, 120, 121, 125, 137, 139, 147
Greene, Kevin, 99
Greenlaw, Dre, 135, 140, 146, 147
Grgich, Visco, 5
Griese, Brian, 143
Griggs, David, 96
Haley, Charles, 59, 68, 74, 85
Hanks, Merton, 90
Harbaugh, Jim, 105, 113, 114, 117, 118, 119, 123, 124, 125, 128, 131
Harbaugh, John, 123
Hardman, Cedrick, 31
Harold, Eli, 129
Harris, David, 68
Hatcher, Teri, 73
Hearst, Garrison, 99, 100, 101, 103
Heisman Trophy, 34, 142
Henke, Ed, 23
Herchman, Bill, 18
Hickey, Red, 22, 23
Hicks, Dwight, 43, 49, 115
Hill, Tyreek, 137
Hollister, Jacob, 135
Holmgren, Mike, 61, 83, 98
Hoyer, Brian, 133
Huey Lewis and the News, 73
Hufanga, Talanoa, 139
Hurts, Jalen, 146
Indianapolis Colts, 98, 101, 113, 128
Iowa State University, 143
Irvin, Michael, 85
Iupati, Mike, 125
James, LaMichael, 123
Jennings, Jauan, 147, 151
Jennings, Stanford, 65
Joe Robbie Stadium, 65, 67, 97
Johnson, Jimmy, 25
Johnson, Jimmy (coach), 87, 93
Johnson, John Henry, 12, 13, 15
Johnson, Josh, 144
Johnson, Pete, 49
Jones, Brent, 60, 69, 90, 156
Jones, Chris, 153
Jones, Jerry, 93
Juszczyk, Kyle, 144, 149, 150
Kaepernick, Colin, 119, 120, 121, 123, 125, 129, 133, 145
Kansas City Chiefs, 33, 86, 87, 89, 134, 136, 137, 142, 150, 152, 153, 154
Kelce, Travis, 134, 150
Kelly, Chip, 128, 129, 132
Kemp, Jeff, 59
Kezar, Mary A., 2
Kezar Stadium, vii, ix, x, 1, 2, 3, 6, 7, 9, 13, 14, 18, 19, 21, 24, 25, 26, 27, 28, 30, 31, 33
Kilmer, Billy, 23, 26
Kittle, George, viii, 90, 133, 134, 137, 144, 145, 147, 150, 165
Kopay, Dave, 27
Krueger, Charlie, 24, 27
Kwalick, Ted, 30, 34
Lakes, Roland, 24
Lambeau Field, 98, 125
Lance, Trey, 139, 142, 143, 145
Landry, Tom, 23, 28
Lane, Bobby, 19
Layden, Elmer, 3
Lee, Amp, 83
Leiser, Bill, 10
Len Eshmont Award, 87, 116
Levi's Stadium, ix, 45, 124, 126, 127, 128, 139, 142, 147, 149
Lewis, Albert, 88
Lilly, Bob, 33
Lincoln Financial Field, 146
Lloyd, Brandon, 112
Lombardi Trophy, ix, 56, 60, 75, 95, 102, 132
Los Angeles Dons, 6
Los Angeles Express, 61
Los Angeles Raiders, 63, 82, 88
Los Angeles Rams, 10, 16, 17, 25, 28, 29, 30, 31, 41, 50, 56, 71, 75, 79, 109, 130, 138, 139, 142
Lott, Ronnie, 42, 43, 49, 59, 65, 70, 73, 79, 81, 82, 90, 117
Louisiana State University, 4
Louisiana Superdome, 76, 77, 123
Love, Jordan, 147
Lynch, John, vii, 132, 133, 142, 143, 150, 154
Mahomes, Patrick, 136, 137, 150, 152, 153
Manning, Archie, 40
Manning, Peyton, 101, 113
Marino, Dan, 52, 55
Mariucci, Steve, 98, 99, 101, 105, 108, 109, 111, 112
Marshall, Jim, 26
McCaffrey, Christian, viii, 57, 130, 142, 144, 145, 146, 147, 149, 150, 151, 153
McCulley, Pete, 35
McDonald, Tim, 99
McElhenny, Hugh, x, 12, 13, 15, 23, 101
McGuire, Dan, 12, 18
McIntyre, Guy, 51
McKinnon, Jerick, 134
McKittrick, Bobb, 75
McKyer, Tim, 68
McPherson, Bill, 75
McVay, John, 75
Means, Natrone, 94
Meyer, Ken, 35
Miami Dolphins, 35, 52, 53, 54, 55, 143
Miami Seahawks, 6
Million Dollar Backfield, 12, 13
Minnesota Vikings, 23, 26, 30, 33, 59, 61, 62, 63, 72, 80, 99
Monday Night Football, 71, 88

Monk, Art, 50
Montana, Joe, ii, 37, 38, 39, 40, 41, 45, 46, 47, 49, 51, 52, 53, 55, 57, 58, 59, 61, 62, 63, 65, 67, 69, 70, 71, 72, 73, 75, 76, 77, 79, 81, 82, 83, 85, 86, 87, 89, 93, 97, 99, 115, 127, 137, 144, 145, 156, 166
Moore, Lenny, 145
Morabito, Jane, 23, 31, 34, 35
Morabito, Josephine, 23, 31, 34, 35
Morabito, Tony, ix, 3, 4, 6, 7, 10, 15, 18, 19, 23, 127, 154
Morabito, Vic, 10, 15, 23
Moroski, Mike, 59
Morze, Frank, x
Moss, Randy, 60
Most Valuable Player (NFL), 21, 29, 49, 65, 75, 83, 137, 139, 146
Mr. Irrelevant, 143, 147
Mullens, Nick, 134
Musburger, Brent, 67
Namath, Joe, 52
National Football Conference (NFC), 31, 33, 37, 63, 90, 93, 95, 125, 131, 146, 147, 149
National Football League (NFL), vii, 3, 5, 7, 10, 11, 12, 16, 19, 21, 23, 26, 27, 29, 30, 31, 35, 37, 38, 39, 40, 43, 50, 51, 52, 56, 57, 59, 60, 69, 73, 75, 79, 82, 83, 87, 88, 92, 98, 101, 102, 105, 106, 107, 111, 117, 118, 119, 124, 127, 129, 133, 134, 135, 139, 140, 142, 143, 145, 150, 154
National Tight Ends Day, 134
New England Patriots, 34, 56, 70, 133
New Orleans Saints, 27, 28, 30, 40, 61, 98, 118, 119, 121, 134
New York Giants, 23, 51, 57, 59, 61, 79, 87, 110, 111, 118
New York Jets, 100, 101
New York Yankees, 6, 8, 9
Newberry, Jeremy, 104
Newhouse, Dave, 13
Newton, Cam, 125
NFC Championship Game, 23, 30, 31, 33, 44, 45, 50, 51, 63, 79, 85, 87, 92, 93, 95, 97, 99, 118, 121, 131, 137, 144, 148, 149, 150, 154
NFC West division, 30, 33, 63, 71, 93, 98, 109, 111, 117, 125
NFL championship, 19
NFL draft, 11, 23, 27, 34, 35, 37, 41, 43, 50, 51, 52, 56, 61, 68, 86, 90, 112, 113, 114, 125, 132, 139, 140, 142, 143
NFL Films, 26
NFL Players Association, 50, 59
Nolan, Dick, 28, 30, 34, 112
Nolan, Mike, 112, 113
Nomellini, Leo, 11, 18
North Dakota State University, 139
Norton, Chico, 45
Norton, Ken Jr., 81, 91, 99
Oakland A's, 70
Oakland Raiders, 34, 35
Oakland Tech, 29
O'Connor, Fred, 35
Offensive Player of the Year, 150
Okeafor, Chike, 111
Olmstead, Michael, 73
Orange Bowl, 117
Owens, James, 37
Owens, R. C., 16, 23
Owens, Terrell, 103, 104, 107, 108, 109, 111
Parks, Dave, 27
Perry, Joe, 5, 7, 9, 10, 11, 12, 13, 15, 23, 90
Philadelphia Eagles, 10, 15, 69, 74, 75, 93, 95, 109, 144, 146
Pick at the Stick, 124
Pittsburgh Steelers, 34, 39, 41, 51, 90
Plummer, Gary, 88, 97
Plunkett, Jim, 34
Policy, Carmen, 98, 102, 113, 115
Polytechnic High School, 19
Pontiac Silverdome, 46, 47, 48, 49
Prescott, Dak, 145
Pro Bowl, 15, 25, 43, 90, 99, 112, 113, 125, 128, 139, 142
Pro Football Hall of Fame, vii, 1, 13, 25, 39, 43, 52, 57, 90, 95, 102, 106, 109, 115, 116, 128
Purdy, Brock, 143, 144, 145, 146, 147, 148, 149, 150, 153, 154, 165
Ramsey, Jalen, 138
Rathman, Tom, 63, 68, 69, 77
Rattay, Tim, 113
Razzano, Tony, 37
Reddick, Hassan, 144
Reid, Eric, 129
Reynolds, Jack "Hacksaw," 49
Rice, Jerry, vi, 56, 57, 59, 60, 61, 62, 63, 64, 65, 67, 69, 71, 77, 78, 79, 85, 87, 88, 95, 97, 98, 99, 107, 124, 145, 165
Riggins, John, 50
Riley, Preston, 33
Robinson, Jackie, 7
Rockne, Knute, 4
Rodgers, Aaron, 113, 121, 139
Rohde, Len, 28, 33
Roman, Greg, 123
Rookie of the Year, 12, 90, 135
Rote, Tobin, 19
Ruffo, Al, ix, 3
Ryan, Buddy, 69
St. Clair, Bob, 14, 19, 25
St. Louis Cardinals, 23, 25
St. Louis Rams, 98, 109, 119
Salata, Paul, 143
Samuel, Deebo, 137, 138, 140, 144, 146, 147, 150
Sanders, Deion, 81, 91, 98
San Diego Chargers, vi, 94, 95, 96, 97
San Francisco Chronicle, 10
San Francisco Examiner, 23
San Francisco Giants, vii, 31, 70
Sandifer, Bill, 31
San Jose State University, 106
Santa Clara University, ix, 3, 4, 5, 90, 127
Sapolu, Jesse, 85
Sapp, Warren, 99
Sayers, Gale, 26
Scully, Vin, 45
Seattle Seahawks, 109, 114, 117, 125, 128, 135, 144
Seau, Junior, 95
Seifert, George, 19, 39, 55, 68, 70, 75, 82, 83, 86, 89, 93, 95, 98
Seubert, Rich, 111
Shanahan, Kyle, vii, 131, 132, 133, 134, 135, 137, 140, 142, 145, 153, 154
Shanahan, Mike, 83, 97, 132
Sharper, Darren, 103
Shaughnessy, Clark, 5
Shaw, Buck, 4, 5, 7, 12, 15
Sherman, Richard, 125, 135
shotgun formation, 22, 23
Shula, Don, 52
Simmons, Lon, 62
Simpson, O. J., 35, 37
Singletary, Mike, 112, 117, 118
Smith, Aldon, 125
Smith, Alex, 113, 117, 118, 119
Smith, Emmitt, 85
Smith, J. D., 19
Smith, Jimmy, 123
Smith, Justin, 112
Smith, Malcolm, 125
Soldier Field, 63
Solomon, Freddie, 40, 45, 51, 56
Soltau, Gordy, 15, 16, 23
Sorrell, Allen, 3, 10

Spadia, Lou, 23, 28, 31, 35
Staley, Joe, 112, 118
Standlee, Norm, 4, 7
Stanford Football Highlights, 36
Stanford Stadium, 53, 55, 70
Stanford University, 5, 34, 36, 105, 115, 117, 132, 142
State Farm Stadium, 139
Staubach, Roger, 33, 85
Stephens, John, 70
Stokes, J. J., 104
Strader, Red, 15
Strahan, Michael, 111
Streets, Tai, 104, 110, 111
Strzykalski, Johnny, 6
Stubblefield, Dana, 99
Sugar Bowl, 4
Sunday Night Football, 145
Super Bowl, ii, vi, vii, ix, 28, 29, 30, 33, 34, 36, 39, 41, 43, 45, 46, 47, 48, 49, 50, 52, 53, 54, 55, 56, 59, 60, 63, 64, 65, 66, 67, 68, 69, 71, 75, 76, 77, 78, 79, 81, 85, 87, 90, 91, 94, 95, 96, 97, 103, 105, 113, 116, 117, 119, 121, 122, 123, 125, 131, 132, 135, 136, 137, 139, 140, 142, 143, 144, 146, 149, 150, 151, 152, 153, 154, 155
Super Bowl V, 30
Super Bowl XVI, ii, 46, 47, 48, 49, 50, 65
Super Bowl XIX, 52, 53, 54, 55
Super Bowl XXIII, 64, 65, 66, 67, 71
Super Bowl XXIV, 76, 77, 78, 97
Super Bowl XXIX, vi, 94, 95, 96, 97, 116
Super Bowl XLVII, 122, 123
Super Bowl LIV, 136, 137, 150
Super Bowl LVIII, 149, 150, 151, 152, 153
Super Bowl MVP, 55, 64, 67, 77
Susoeff, Nick, 7
Swift, Taylor, 150
Switzer, Barry, 93
T formation, 5, 12
Tampa Bay Buccaneers, vii, 59, 61, 75, 79, 99, 112, 143, 145
Taylor, John, 66, 67, 68, 69, 71, 79, 87, 89
Teague, George, 109
Terrell, Pat, 103
Thesz, Lou, 11
Thomas, Joe, 35, 36, 37
Thomas, Solomon, 132
Thrailkill, Larry, 102
Tittle, Y. A., 12, 13, 16, 17, 18, 19, 23, 29
Tomsula, Jim, 128, 132
Toneff, Bob, 14
Towle, Ali, 131
Turner, Keena, 70, 81
Turre, Ernie, 10
Twombly, Wells, 23
Tyler, Wendell, 50, 51
Unitas, Johnny, 52
United States Football League (USFL), 61
University of California, Berkeley (Cal Berkeley), 4, 113
University of California, Los Angeles (UCLA), 37
University of Iowa, 134
University of Michigan, 128
University of Minnesota, 11
University of Notre Dame, 4, 37, 83, 90
University of Oklahoma, 93
University of San Francisco, 25
University of Southern California (USC), 43
Veterans Stadium, 69
Vildor, Kindle, 149
Walker, Delanie, 117
Wallace, Steve, 97
Walls, Everson, 45
Walsh, Bill, vii, 36, 37, 38, 39, 40, 41, 43, 45, 46, 49, 50, 51, 52, 55, 56, 57, 59, 61, 63, 65, 67, 68, 69, 75, 77, 89, 95, 105, 106, 107, 115, 127
Ward, Arch, 3
Warner, Fred, 135, 140, 141, 145, 147, 150
Warner House, The, 145, 160
Warner, Pop, 9, 22, 115
Washington, Gene, 2, 29, 34
Washington Redskins, 10, 32, 33, 50, 79, 140
Washington, Vic, 34
Watters, Ricky, 81, 87, 90, 92, 96, 97, 98
Wersching, Ray, 40, 49
West Coast offense, 36, 51, 115
White, Reggie, 69
Wilcox, Dave, 25
Williams, Delvin, 34
Williamson, Carlton, 43
Williams, Trent, 140, 142, 150, 153
Willig, Matt, 104
Willis, Patrick, 121, 125, 128
Wilson, Billy, 15, 16, 18, 19
Wilson, Mike, 62, 81
Wilson, Russell, 135
Witcher, Dick, 30
Woodall, Lee, 99
Woods, Ickey, 65
Woodson, Rod, 99
World Series, 70
World War II, 11
Wright, Eric, 43, 49, 70, 81
Wyche, Sam, 36, 37, 65, 67
Yonamine, Kaname "Wally," 7
York, Denise DeBartolo, 102, 105, 117, 127
York, Jed, 105, 117, 124, 127, 128, 131, 132, 154
York, John, 102, 105, 112, 117, 127
Young, Bryant, 81, 90, 99, 116
Young, Steve, vii, 59, 61, 62, 65, 67, 70, 79, 80, 81, 82, 83, 85, 86, 87, 88, 89, 93, 97, 98, 99, 101, 103, 105, 106, 115, 124, 137, 145, 165

ACKNOWLEDGMENTS

Thank you to Steve Young, Ted Atlas, Dan Brown, Jim Gensheimer, the late Jerry Green, Martin Jacobs, Terrell Lloyd, Brad Mangin, Kevin Moore, Nadia Nasr, Dave Newhouse, Michael Olmstead, Kirk Reynolds, the late Al Ruffo, Tracy Seipel, Mark Soltau, Shelby Soltau, Keena Turner, Jerry Walker, Michael Zagaris . . . plus always and forever, Barbara Purdy. —MP

Thank you to Beryl Love, Jeremy Suess, Kristin Suess, and Dashiell Suess. —JS

COURTESY OF DINO VOURNAS/AFP VIA GETTY IMAGES

COURTESY OF BRIAN ROTHMULLER/ICON SPORTSWIRE VIA GETTY IMAGES

COURTESY OF GEORGE GOJKOVICH/GETTY IMAGES